# gardening for
# small spaces

# gardening for
# small spaces

Clever design solutions to make the most of your plot

## John Cushnie

METRO BOOKS
NEW YORK

*To Evie Iseult, a much loved little granddaughter*

Project editor: Jennifer Wheatley
Designer: Louise Leffler
Illustrations: John Cushnie (except for pages 4 and 105; Alison Clements)
Copy editor: Penny Phillips
Picture researcher: Julia Gelpke
Production director: Sha Huxtable
Americanizer: Trevor Cole

Metro Books
122 Fifth Avenue
New York, NY 10011

ISBN: 978-1-4351-2112-6

A Catalog In Publication record for this title is available from the Library of Congress.

Color reproduction by Scanhouse
Printed in Singapore

10 9 8 7 6 5 4 3 2 1

# contents

# Introduction

Small is usually beautiful—but then I'm over 6ft tall! The thing is, it is easier to make a small garden beautiful. Throughout this book you will see exciting and inspirational examples of small and even tiny gardens that are to die for.

The quest for building land has never been greater, and with conditions for planning approval being tightened more and more, houses, apartments and town houses are being shoehorned into a given space. Where the existing gardens are large, new developments all too often sprout up suddenly like mushrooms to cover the old tennis court or vegetable garden.

At the same time, more and more people are taking up gardening. Fresh, tasty, and, in many cases, organic fruit and vegetables are being grown. The garden has become the place of choice for entertaining: before-dinner drinks, alfresco dining or the ubiquitous barbecue releasing the dubious fragrance of burnt hamburger into the surrounding gardens.

It is a great place for children to play, safe and secure from the outside world and in view from at least one window. There will be a favorite sheltered and screened spot, just made for that break for a shared pot of coffee and a bit of gossip. It's also ideal for gardening!

Not all gardens have soil to garden in—but don't let that hold you back. Where there is reasonable access, a basement garden is a dream come true. It will be sheltered, with lots of vertical space for climbers and wall plants. Maintenance will be low, allowing you more time to enjoy your bijou garden. A balcony, irrespective of size, takes on a new life when furnished with plants, becoming an "outdoor room". Rooftop gardens are very "in", making every one of your friends want to visit

and share the experience. City and town courtyards with only a small area on either side of the entrance will need careful landscaping. All of them will comprise hard surfaces requiring imported soil in containers or raised beds. Even without the benefit of open ground to plant into, it is still possible to grow excellent crops of fruit and vegetables, and have a riot of color from shrubs, perennials, bulbs, annuals, and small trees. Containers range from wooden half-barrels, glazed pots, woven hazel stems, and natural stone troughs to metal and plastic. There are soil mixes to suit every type of plant, from ericaceous for lime-haters to soil-based for permanent shrubs.

An enclosed, small garden has an intimate feeling that is difficult to achieve in larger spaces. Plants with fragrant foliage and flowers will add to the experience, while evergreen plants will provide a "wrap-around" secure feeling. Sunbathing while those above and around your garden are oblivious of your existence can be gratifying, reinforcing your love of your own little space. If it is possible to grow and train climbers to form a living canopy, then a part of your garden can provide an ideal spot for a romantic evening for two.

As well as being more intimate, the small garden makes it easier to generate a "feel-good" factor. Sitting close to ripening fruit and your own vegetables ready to harvest can encourage smugness—and rightly so. Watching your carefully selected plants successfully thriving in spite of deep shade or hard-baked, dry soil proves that you are in every sense a gardener.

Oh, there are many advantages to gardening in a small space—not least that for older and less fit gardeners the small size is ideal. Those with a disability may be able to enjoy

LEFT: *An intimate screened and sheltered, low-maintenance garden—the ideal spot for relaxing with a glass of wine or cup of coffee.*

limited gardening without the whole thing getting out of hand.

As fewer man-hours will be expended on the maintenance of a small area, small gardens are also great for people leading busy lives. In an era when both partners may spend their day working, there is little time to look after a large garden. Weekends and holidays are often spent away from home rather than in the garden. To employ part-time labor is expensive, and the quality of work by non-professionals may leave a lot to be desired.

Inner cities and large towns are also more prone to atmospheric pollution and high levels of unwanted noise. The garden, no matter how small, can seriously help to reduce both these types of pollution. The shoots, stems, and leaves of trees and shrubs filter and trap dust and help to muffle sound. Outdoor spaces in large built-up areas are essential to the well-being of our environment. Leafy plants absorb carbon dioxide, adding oxygen to the atmosphere. Birds rely on plants for food, and even the pests associated with plants are an important part of the food chain. A wide range of flowering trees and shrubs means a continuing supply of nectar for bees. In large cities and towns every single garden, no matter how small, aids the survival of birds, bees, butterflies, and other insects.

I started by saying that small is beautiful, and that is so true of gardens. Gardeners and non-gardeners alike are more likely to enthuse over a well-designed, well-executed, and well-maintained small garden than when confronted with a spacious, spread-out garden. There is literally no room for mistakes. The attention to detail, range of plants used, clever use of the smallest space, and feeling of being part of the whole garden area give both the gardener and the visitor a feeling of well-being.

TOP: *A comfortable seat surrounded by plants.*
BOTTOM: *Al fresco breakfast on the deck.*

# What size is a small garden?

It is all relative! In rural areas where land is less expensive than in the inner city, a so-called small garden could actually be quite large. On the other hand, I have landscaped inner-city basements and back yards where the total available space has been less than 30sq ft. The average small back garden is probably somewhere in the region of 150-200sq ft, giving a width of approximately 20ft and a length of 25ft.

Front gardens as small as 100sq ft can be made interesting and inviting with year-round color, while still allowing space to park the car securely off road and close to the front door.

Then there are keen gardeners with no flower beds at all, who make do with window boxes, pots, and containers, nevertheless managing to provide the kitchen with fresh vegetables, fruit, and flowers while giving a display of color throughout the four seasons.

# Inspiration

One way to kick-start inspirational designs is to visit other gardens and adapt what pleases you to your situation. You can get some great ideas from books and magazines.

However, always imagine how the pretty-picture garden might look after a few years. Don't be conned by those marvelously colorful, interesting, and inspirational gardens constructed as show gardens—often designed to look good for a particular, limited time. Plants are packed in with no consideration as to their eventual height or spread. Within days everything has been removed and sold off or sent back to the nursery. The instant show garden is for the short term only.

Your garden will take time to mature, but during that time it will provide endless enjoyment for all involved. It will be a constant source of entertainment, amusement, surprise, and, above all, satisfaction.

By the time it is mature and almost exactly how you want it, you will know every plant in it, each plant's needs and how to get the best from all of them. That is what gardening is all about; size truly doesn't matter.

RIGHT: *Even the smallest garden will accommodate a wide range of plants and provide color, shape, and texture, while also offering privacy.*
FAR RIGHT: *These plants provide interest all the way to the front door, while the change of surface underfoot makes the journey seem longer.*

# Part I: creative ideas and design

*Ways to get the most out of your garden and give the illusion of space.*

# Chapter 1—
# What have you got?

It is crucial to become totally familiar with your garden—and I don't mean just knowing its size and shape. If you are going to get the best out of it you will have to feel at home in the space. Feel the wind, see where the sun shines on your face; shiver in the shade and be aware of the lie of the land. Look at it out of every window possible, and then look back at the windows from every corner of the garden.

Gradually you will fine-tune your ideas and before you put pen to paper you will know what is possible and practical.

# Types of small garden

## BASEMENT GARDENS

Basement gardens are often, frustratingly for the gardener, full of dense shade; the sun may manage to shine only on the top one third of one or two of the walls. However, despite that tiny moan they are great fun to design and to garden in. There are generally lots of walls, often quite high and sometimes with the benefit of railings on top. These allow you to introduce more vigorous climbers than the space would suggest. Plant selection is critical, the confined space usually having to accommodate a door, a window (perhaps two) and sometimes a flight of steps. If a single plant outgrows its space it will cause problems. Yet in the confined space it is easy with a few plants to transform the basement garden into a perfume factory.

## BACK YARDS

Designing a garden in the back yard of a terraced house can be tricky. It often requires considerable thought and several attempts before you settle for the right mix of plant material. The floor area may be only a few square feet, with double that area of 6ft-high walls. The potential garden will therefore be in shade, cold, and probably with a concrete floor. But transforming a back yard into a bijou garden is not only a challenge, it is also a joy to undertake, with enormous job satisfaction when the garden is a success.

The number-one priority is to increase the available reflected daylight by painting the walls white or cream. Where the ground is being surfaced, use light-colored tiles or slabs and introduce white gravel. Wall plants such as climbers will need support and should not be too vigorous. Clematis prefer their roots and lower stems to be in shade, with the top growth and flowers in full sun, so they are ideal for the back yard.

The really good news for back-yard gardeners is that it is possible to get on top of slugs and snails. Before the plants and soil are introduced the numbers of these pests can be greatly reduced, while follow-up checks along with a few friendly robins will keep the recurrence low.

Surrounded by walls, these gardens do not require you to design in privacy or shelter; all the space may be devoted to making the surroundings aesthetically pleasing.

OPPOSITE: *Compact basement garden, with just enough space for two seats among the plants.*
BELOW: *A delightful back yard with a massive selection of plants and space to entertain.*

## FRONT GARDENS

The front gardens of many inner-city properties have been largely converted to hard-surface concrete, tarmac, or gravel in order to provide off-street parking. While accepting the need for somewhere to park and sympathizing with house and business owners, I maintain that there is still the opportunity to garden around the parking space.

Surface the parking zone with materials such as gravel or porous tiles that allow rain to percolate through rather than run off into drains that are already under pressure. Where there is space, even a 12in-wide border in front of a boundary fence will accommodate lots of plants to provide year-round interest and color. Pots of plants at the front door will be welcoming to visitors. A timber or wrought-iron arch at the front door with pot-grown roses, honeysuckle or jasmine will add height to the planting.

Where it is not possible to open gates outwards, consider a sliding gate that takes up less space and allows the rear of the vehicle to be just inside the entrance.

Some small gardens are ridiculously narrow. The side entrance to a house may be a strip just 6–9ft wide between the house wall and the neighbouring wall or fence. The only access path may be along this long, narrow pass. It is invariably shaded, perhaps never visited by the sun. The ground may be concreted, with manholes and inspection chambers, and, to add to the misery, at least one wall is probably cluttered with downpipes and gutters. With some knowledge of plants and a bit of design flair, you can transform this awkward site into a gem of a garden—with the advantage that you have a captive audience. Everyone has to take the "long walk" to the front door, so they have time to enjoy your design and choice of plants.

## ROOF TERRACES AND BALCONIES

I have never landscaped a rooftop or balcony that was warm. There are plenty of days and even weeks when such places can be ideal for sunbathing, but for part of the year they often do suffer from wind and cold draughts. Bear this in mind when selecting plants. If they have to remain outside all year round, avoid planting tender plants and choose species that look good for most of the year. A balcony garden will always be in view from inside, so you have the opportunity to impress visitors and encourage them to go out for a better look, even in winter. Some plants, such as the New Zealand Cabbage Palm, *Cordyline australis,* look tropical and tend to give an impression of warmth, yet are hardy enough for most rooftop gardens. Low-growing deciduous shrubs and herbaceous perennials that keep their heads below the parapet do well on roofs, either in containers or raised beds.

There are properties, especially in inner cities, that have no garden at all. Where big houses have been converted into apartments, often only those on the ground floor and in the basement have access to outside space. What others may have is a set of steps up or down to their front or rear door. A flight of steps could hardly be described as a garden, but where needs must, it should be possible to grow some plants.

RIGHT: *A well-screened front garden.*
FAR RIGHT: *Colorful balcony plants in containers, to be replaced in winter with tough flowering heathers.*
OPPOSITE: *"Room at the top" with established shrubs and climbers.*

# Position of the garden

Earlier on I was keen that before starting to design you spend some time in the garden, getting the feel of it. Part of "getting acquainted" is becoming familiar with the climatic conditions. Are there areas that are in shade—and if so, for how long? The condition of the ground will determine whether it is dry shade or wet shade. Don't worry; either way there are lots of suitable plants. What part faces the sun during the afternoon? Are there areas that get sun all day long? Mark down the points of the compass on a plan. If the garden is exposed to the elements, it may need some form of shelter. Where the wind is being channelled between buildings or high fences, consider designing in a tough evergreen shrub such as *Viburnum tinus* 'Spring Bouquet' to filter the wind.

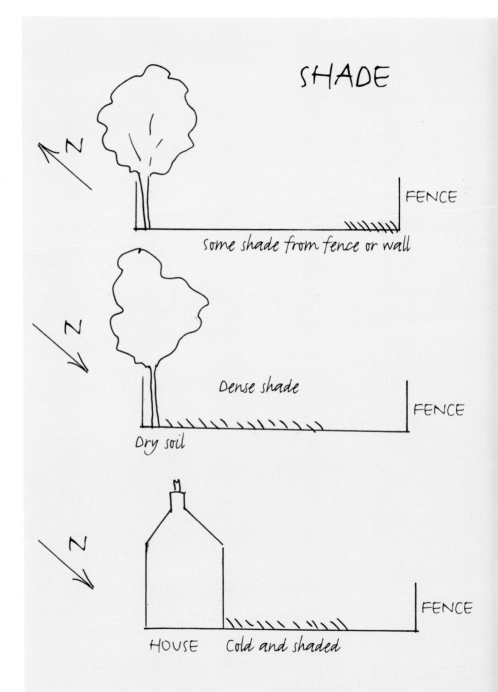

SHADE

some shade from fence or wall

FENCE

Dense shade

FENCE

Dry soil

HOUSE    Cold and shaded

FENCE

RIGHT: *If you know where north is, you can work out where there will be shaded areas in the garden.*
OPPOSITE: *On a warm summer afternoon, a little shade will be welcome.*

# A solution for every position

### North-facing

North-facing sites in the northern hemisphere will be without sunlight, shaded, and colder. While lots of plants will survive and thrive, others won't tolerate cold wet soil. Such conditions are ideal for slugs and snails, so constant vigilance will be necessary to keep them in check. Concentrate on plants and on the possibility of using the space to store garbage cans or fuel tanks and to house a composting area. Plants such as clematis that like a cool root run can be planted on the north side and trained around a corner to flower on a west- or east-facing wall. Plants for north-facing balconies will have to be tough. Where winters are severe, the soil in containers becomes colder than the ground, so choose plants that are at least two zones hardier than where you live. Regular tying in of climbers will prevent their being damaged by strong winds.

### South-facing

South-facing sites will be warm with the possibility of full sun—ideal for sunbathing and for growing fruit. In the early afternoon, summer sun will make the area uncomfortably hot; a suitable small tree sited between the sitting area and the sun will afford you an area of warm but welcome shade. In case of a sudden cold spell, tender plants are easier to manage and protect if they are in containers. These may be moved to a more sheltered position and covered with a layer of horticultural fleece. Where there isn't the space for a small patio or deck area, a garden seat positioned to face the sun will be a luxury and a blessing.

### East-facing

For morning coffee and a quick read of the morning paper, an east-facing patio is ideal! However, where the garden faces east there is the risk of a late spring frost coupled with the early-morning sun damaging flowers and young spring shoots. Camellia blooms are particularly susceptible. Easterly winds can be cold; a suitably placed clipped, evergreen yew tree will protect the area around a garden seat while adding height to the garden.

### West-facing

Gardens facing west enjoy late-afternoon and evening sun and are the place to be for a pre-dinner glass of wine with friends. West-facing walls that are sheltered are ideal for growing trained fruit trees and shrubs that are not fully hardy. The soil will tend to dry out, so you might opt for a Mediterranean garden with plants that love warm, dry conditions.

# Making the most of the microclimate

Usually city and large town gardens are warmer than those in the country and the additional few degrees are of enormous benefit to the keen grower. You will be able to try plants that outside the immediate area would require greenhouse or conservatory protection.

As gardeners we tend to take chances and are proud of managing to grow "tricky" plants despite adverse weather and soil conditions. We all know what hardy means, and the difference between hardy, half-hardy and tender, but we tend to ignore that information for the opportunity of growing something unusual or challenging—or just to be one-up on our gardening friends. Inner-city basement gardens are often totally frost-free, allowing all sorts of tender plants to be grown.

# Assessing soil quality and pH

If the site is new, are weeds growing well (good soil) or are they stunted and miserable with yellowing leaves (infertile or very wet soil)?

Dig a few holes and check the quality of the top foot of soil. Is it heavy, sticky clay, wet, or dry? None of these is ideal, but all of them can be improved and be the base of a good garden. If the soil is a dark gray-black without any fiber, it may have been gardened for the last century and, as a result, be deficient in every nutrient and full of plant pests and diseases.

Whether yours is an existing garden or a new site there will be indicators of what you, and your plants, will have to deal with. Where rhododendrons, camellias, and other ericaceous plants are thriving, the soil must be acid. If ceanothus, pinks and lilac are common and doing well, the ground is likely to be alkaline. A good indicator of acid or alkaline soil is the color of established florist's hydrangeas: if the flowers are blue or purple, the soil is acidic; pink or red denotes alkaline conditions. Where there are no plants to give you a clue, look in neighboring gardens and see what is doing well.

A soil test using a good analysis kit will give you the pH reading. These kits are available from garden centers and stores. Don't be tempted to buy a cheap one. At best they are inaccurate and at worst they don't work at all. It's frustrating if the soil sample produces a color that isn't even on the color chart!

Take readings from various parts of the garden. An accurate reading above 7 means that your soil is alkaline; below 7 means your soil is acid. I am happy to work with either. An acid soil will suit ericaceous plants such as rhododendrons, camellias, and pieris. An alkaline soil will allow you to grow wonderful specimens of shrubs such as lilac and ceanothus. Adding lime will raise the pH, making the soil more alkaline. When vegetable crops are grown in rotation, lime is applied to the bed where brassicas are being grown; these will use up most of the lime leaving the ground suitable for other crops the following year. In truth, a neutral soil will give you and your plants the most scope for variety.

# Surfaces

As hard surfaces go, a concrete floor is a cheap option and invariably an uninspiring surface. Just because the previous owner or the builder took the easy way out and concreted the garden there is no reason for you to accept its inevitability. Check with the neighbors and find out why it was made hard-surface. There may be a good reason, such as that the garden overlies a sheet of rock or there's an absence of soil. The last occupant may have kept dogs in kennels and found concrete easiest to clean. Perhaps the previous owner hated gardening!

If in the past a small area was constantly dug up by your friendly urban skunk or raccoon, laying concrete or slabs was probably a last-ditch effort to thwart the destruction. You may have to live with the concrete and garden in containers; where there is a lack of soil it can be imported, though this can be very pricey, and time-consuming where there is no proper access.

Let's agree that the concrete has to stay but become invisible: where the entrances and steps allow you to raise the level, the best option is to resurface on top of the existing concrete with gravel, tiles, or natural stone slabs. Breaking the concrete base will allow water to drain away more quickly, but the surface may heave in winter in cold regions.

# Levels and slopes

Is the site level or sloping? Where the site slopes, consider how this may affect any hard surfaces or construction work such as a patio, water feature or pergola. It is difficult to level a portion of a small garden without forming steep banks or retaining walls. Do take accurate levels. You will be amazed how much the ground drops. Use wooden pegs, a straight length of timber and a spirit level. Drive a peg into the ground at the highest point and level across using the timber and spirit level to another peg. Drive this in until the bubble in the level settles in the center of the glass.

# Fences and old walls

Are perimeter fences high and solid? Perhaps the neighbors are unfriendly—or perhaps they are too friendly. A fence may be essential as a barrier to noise or high winds or simply to offer some privacy. Fences may have been erected to deter neighboring cats and dogs from trespassing.

Old natural stone walls must not be ripped down or hidden. They speak of the almost forgotten art of craftsmen's building skills, where manpower and nature often produced superior results to modern machinery and man-made materials. Sandstone and limestone give the impression of warmth. Wall shrubs and climbers should simply break up the overall view of the wall while allowing its beauty to be complemented by the plants. Red- or blue-flowering shrubs will succeed with a pale yellow or buff stone surface, while against the same surface cream or yellow flowers will tend to disappear.

ABOVE: *A stone wall, partially covered by plants, has a natural look.*
OPPOSITE: *Hydrangea color is a good indicator of soil type: blue for acid, pink for alkaline.*

# Chapter 2—
# What do you want?

When you have assessed what you've got, decide what you want from your garden. What are the most important elements?

Once you put pen to paper you will find that you are full of ideas. Is it the daily pleasure of gardening you are after, or once your garden is landscaped are you content to sit and watch it grow and mature? Will it be used to entertain— and if so, will you require lots of standing space, a barbecue and seats? Comfort and screening may be more important than lots of space. Where there are children, some form of play area or activity zone will almost always be essential; it will need to be safe and in view from a window.

Are there any specialist plants that you wish to grow, such as alpines, bog plants, perennials, trees, shrubs, fruit, or vegetables? Do you want a cutting border from which flowers may be taken for display in the house without the whole garden being stripped bare? What about a lawn? Do lawns have a place in a small garden where their constant maintenance is a problem and the area is too small for play or entertaining? Where will you store the mower?

Will there be space for a greenhouse? If there is space, enormous fun can be had from this smallest of houses. You can propagate plants from seed and cuttings, grow some of your own tomatoes, cucumbers, melons, peppers, or eggplants. The greenhouse will be useful for overwintering a few tender plants that need frost protection; if it's to be used for this you will need to consider water and electricity supply. It will need to be installed in a sunny, sheltered position away from any children's play area. A path leading from the house to the greenhouse will be beneficial. If there is not the space for a greenhouse, consider a cold frame for overwintering some plants.

# Style

This is an opportunity to customize your garden. Would you like it to be formal, with straight lines for paths and patio and lots of dwarf clipped box hedges? Perhaps you are looking for a leafy, jungle-like effect where shades of green and leaf shape are the main interest. Or how about a garden that suggests hotter climates or is a reminder of holidays abroad, with palms, olive trees, and pot-grown flowering *Strelitzia reginae* (bird of paradise)? You could even have a seaside theme, where the sandy "beach" makes the ideal surface for the deck chair.

## COTTAGE-STYLE GARDEN

Living in the inner city should not prevent you from having a cottage-style garden. The smaller the garden, the easier it will be to manage and maintain elements that, on a larger scale, would require a lot of time. This type of garden is suited to either the front or the rear—and the more walls the better, for growing plants on and against.

It will be possible to design such a garden in a shaded area, although this will be less appealing than in a position of full sun. Larger areas may be gravelled or paved, with random planting reinforced by self-seeded offspring. *Alchemilla mollis* (lady's mantle), *Aquilegia* (columbine), and all the many species of *Helleborus* (hellebore) look the part and, whether you want them to or not, will scatter seedlings all over the garden to germinate in the most unlikely spots. Towering flowering stems of foxgloves, delphiniums, and hollyhocks, along with mullein and lupin, will further contribute to the cottage atmosphere.

Trained fruit trees vying with climbing and rambling roses for space on sunny walls are also authentic in style.

Timber arches covered with fragrant climbing and rambling roses over paths and around the door will never be out of place, and vegetables mingling with flowering shrubs give a natural feel. Rows of *Dianthus* (pinks) with their scent of cloves and *Primula* 'Wanda' (reddish-purple-flowered primrose) to edge the path will look the part.

Old-fashioned timber picket fencing with the round-topped strips of wood has become fashionable. Painted white with lavender, geranium, and columbines trying to escape through the vertical gaps, it can seal the cottage look.

## WOODLAND GARDEN

It is perfectly possible to have a small woodland garden. There may not be many plants but cleverly designed paths will allow you to meander in several directions making the area seem larger. Use composted bark mulch for the paths and keep them narrow, single file being the walk. Select trees that won't become too large or ones such as the evergreen oak, *Quercus ilex,* which may be pruned to remain compact. Trees with colored bark (*Betula utilis* var. *jacquemontii*) or peeling bark (*Acer griseum*) add interest. Shrubs to fill the gaps between the tree trunks include the shade-loving camellias and skimmia. The woodland floor may be carpeted with spring bulbs such as winter aconites, hardy cyclamen and bluebells. Overhead, wild woodbine (honeysuckle) may be allowed to scamper through the tree branches.

TOP: *Borders and walkways overflowing with flowering plants give a cottage-garden appearance.*
BOTTOM: *Large leafy palms and ferns have a tropical look that seems to raise the temperature.*

## WILDLIFE GARDEN

In the same way as it is possible to have a small woodland area in all but the tiniest of gardens, you can make your garden wildlife-friendly by setting aside a small plot as a wildlife garden. Beneficial insects can be encouraged to take up residence and multiply there. It will be a useful refuge, especially in the inner-city garden, for small mammals, birds, and butterflies. Wild flowers will look pretty in bloom while providing habitat for friendly insects such as butterflies, ladybugs, hoverflies, and lacewings.

Being a tiny corner of an already small plot, your wildlife garden may manage to incorporate only a few of the best habitats—perhaps a single, regularly contained, clump of nettles to provide food for caterpillars. Or a mini pile of old decaying logs might become home to beetles, and provide a sheltered place for overwintering butterflies.

When designing with plants you will naturally select many that are great for wildlife. Ornamental trees and shrubs with berries will provide winter food; seed heads will be another source. Hedges will become building sites for small birds and provide shelter. Ivy that is allowed to grow to maturity will provide winter nectar and food.

By all means encourage birds with nesting boxes, food, and a bird-bath—but a small word of caution. Where fruit is concerned, birds can be very destructive. This is chiefly a problem on soft fruits, currants, raspberries, etc. You may need to net the trees and bushes in winter as well as in summer for the ripening fruit.

I admit to having a love-hate relationship with our feathered friends. I grow trees such as *Sorbus* for their beautiful clusters of late-summer and fall berries. Seldom do I get a glimpse of the ripening berries before the trees shake with flocks of birds devouring the lot. Being a big softie I then put out food to see the birds through the winter.

If you can find space in the shrub bed for a cultivar of *Buddleja davidii,* butterflies will flock to your garden. These are vigorous, large shrubs that benefit from pruning hard back to the older wood every spring. Unfortunately, this shrub seeds freely and it should not be planted in country gardens where it may escape into the surrounding woodlands. *Verbena bonariensis* will take up less space, flowering from summer through fall, and is likewise loved by butterflies. This is a perennial in the south, but a self-seeding annual where winters are cooler.

A wildlife garden is a great way of introducing biodiversity to the city garden. It is also an opportunity for children—the next generation of gardeners—to learn about nature's way of sorting out problems and finding a balance within the garden, while enjoying the sight and sounds of local wildlife.

ABOVE: *Birds and butterflies don't need much space to enjoy the garden.*

## A GARDEN FOR CHILDREN

A safe environment for children is a prerequisite for the family garden. It is great to be able to let them play outside in the fresh air in all weathers. Wearing the right clothes, they never seem to mind the cold or wet in the way adults do. Because children are naturally curious, being outside will often also spark their interest in growing and gardening—another good enough reason for setting aside a small area for their enjoyment.

Design the play area in a position close to the house and easily in view from a ground-floor window. If children can be checked regularly without it seeming obvious they will become confident.

Safety of children has to be the number-one priority. There is no excuse for inappropriate design, poor construction, or inferior materials. There should be no trip hazards or sharp edges.

The garden, or the play part of it, will need to be escape-proof. Use fencing such as 3ft-high wooden picket-type, stained or painted so that it blends in. The gate needs to be fitted with a child-proof lock, as high up as possible and preferably on the outside of the gate. Rooftop gardens and balconies will need to be fitted with barrier railings that can't be climbed upon.

Water features must be 100 percent safe with absolutely no risk of drowning. It is possible to have the sound and sight of water under such conditions, but if you are unhappy with the idea of this, don't construct a water feature until the children are grown up.

Where the patio surface is level, there is less risk of tripping. Both a patio and a deck area may double up as a play area, complete with sunken sand-pit, which must have a waterproof cover to prevent it from being used as a toilet area by animals. A cover also keeps the sand dry during wet weather.

Where older children have the run of the garden, make sure it is safe for play, with no sharp objects or gardening tools left lying about. Lock the shed and greenhouse.

Check your planting list and make sure that within the play area there are no toxic plants or any that cause allergic reactions. Spiny and thorny plants should also be excluded. No poisonous plants, seeds, berries, or fruit. (See page 73.)

Try to include a den where children can safely play while thinking they are hidden from view. A surround of bushy shrubs with a hollow center will do nicely. Having to crawl into the hide is all part of the adventure. It will become a fort, castle, dungeon, and house as their imagination runs riot. It also takes up less space than a purpose-built playhouse.

Encourage children—by example is often best—to sow seeds and grow fruit and vegetables. Give them a small plot of their own, and make sure the soil is fine and easily worked. There seems to be this notion that young children love growing the tallest sunflower. Their dads might—but why would children get excited about something that is much bigger than themselves? Give them seed of dwarf sunflowers that will produce big, happy flowers down at their level.

## ENTERTAINING

Most gardens are not just for admiring. They are there for the enjoyment and pleasure of you and your family or friends. Enough space for seats and a small table is essential, but in reality these don't take up much space. An area 9ft by 6ft will accommodate a small table, three chairs and sufficient leg-room for people to relax with a leisurely glass of wine or for a snooze.

Open-air garden entertaining can be at several levels. There is the chat, gossip and cup of coffee with a friend. There is the party night when teenagers descend on the garden, listen to loud music and make a lot of noise. A stroll along the garden paths with a few friends enjoying a glass of wine before supper is relaxing. Barbecues are great on a balmy evening when the weather is settled. Then there is business entertaining, when deals are made, potential staff sounded out, or information exchanged.

If the garden is well maintained with lots of interest and color, those to be entertained will be at ease or, at the very least, impressed. Comfortable outdoor furniture is desirable, with a table that doesn't rock on an uneven surface. A suitably large umbrella or awning is useful in case it rains. Space to stand chatting other than on the patio is an advantage when there are more than a few couples.

Containers filled with fragrant, flowering plants and perfumed climbers overhead are conducive to an enjoyable time that leaves your friends with pleasant memories.

ABOVE: *I bet the neighbors love to visit!*
OPPOSITE: *Curiosity will encourage children to become gardeners.*

# Making use of what you have and working with limitations

As well as many advantages, there are a few problems commonly associated with small spaces (as mentioned in Chapter 1), which you will need to take into consideration. However, many of these lead to inspired and creative solutions.

The problem I am most frequently asked to resolve is that of a lack of privacy. In cities and towns, the garden is often overlooked by higher buildings. Apartments and their balconies may be directly above your outside space, making a covered-in garden a natural desire.

Boundary fences may be low, offering little in the way of privacy from the gardens on either side.

Basement gardens at the front of a property may be overlooked by every passing pedestrian. Your balcony may face directly into another balcony at a higher or lower level.

In every case it is possible, with limited space, to offer shelter, privacy, and screening. Where you and your garden are being overlooked from above, a simple patio umbrella in the right position is often sufficient to block the view. A snow-white canvas awning stretched like a horizontal sail on stainless-steel wire or hemp rope from three painted or stained timber posts, and angled to allow the sun to shine in, is a wonderfully chic piece of equipment, yet allows your modesty to remain intact.

Where boundary fences are low, you can provide additional height by growing espalier-trained, evergreen pyracantha up the fence with the upper horizontal tiers of branches supported on galvanized or plastic-covered wires.

Extending the upright posts with concave and convex shaped trellis fencing panels will add an extra 12–18in to the height, and when covered with clematis or honeysuckle these will block outsiders' view of your garden.

The desire to screen your basement garden is often in competition with the need for daylight. By allowing evergreen plants such as *Clematis armandii* and *Lonicera henryii* (honeysuckle) to grow up and through the railing along the footpath, you can, with pruning, train a hedge-like barrier that keeps pedestrians away from the railing and prevents their seeing through to your garden.

Balconies are difficult to make private, but an electric overhead awning will offer protection from a higher level. A few tall bamboo or palm plants in containers suitably positioned will help to screen part of the sitting area.

If the garden is in full sun, you may like to have a shady area or simply somewhere to put a lounger out of direct sunlight; often the solution is to design into the planting scheme a single tree positioned between the afternoon sun and the seat. The tree doesn't need to be evergreen or very tall, providing its shadow falls on the right spot.

Lack of space for plants is a common complaint among gardeners. No matter how large the garden, there is never enough space for all the plants. But after a while, we all tend to become more

selective with our plants and buy only those best suited to the garden and the climatic and soil conditions. Knowing the spread of the plant and planting accordingly will prevent the garden from becoming overcrowded and a tangled mess where only the fittest survives.

You are likely to need somewhere to store gardening equipment and patio furniture. For this you can buy ready-made boxes and small lightweight alloy garden sheds; these can be screened with plants or a flowering hedge.

A boot scraper and umbrella stand outside the entrance to the dwelling will reduce the risk of anyone transporting the garden soil and rain into the house.

If the garden is on a slope, are steps going to work or are ramps needed? Steps can add interest to the smallest of gardens. They allow for a change of level and afford a good vantage point from which to look over the garden. Where they are wide enough, pots of plants or vegetables may be positioned at the edge of each step. A gently sloping ramp will allow passage for the wheelbarrow.

Is there a need for surface drainage—and if so, is there any outlet for run-off? If the wet area of ground is small and local, it is better to add a bog garden to your design and allow the run-off from the rest of the garden so it remains moist at all times. Where there is no natural outlet for the drain, excavating a large sump and filling it with stones will mean the drained water is stored underground until it can soak away.

RIGHT: *This is a spot where I would choose to relax. It is private, comfortable, and sheltered.*

# Chapter 3— Landscaping your space

One of the most enjoyable exercises in designing a garden is deciding what features you want. Occasionally, clients tell me to go ahead and do whatever I think best! But that way they would end up with my favorite garden, not theirs. Once I focus the client's attention on their likes and dislikes, they suddenly realize that they do know exactly which features they would like included.

As gardeners, we always want to see more features in the garden but we are, unfortunately, limited by the boundaries.

In the small garden, the fundamental question is: if the feature has to be truly tiny, is it really worth including it? Where the lawn space has to be less than 6–7sq ft, will it add anything to the garden? It certainly won't allow you to play soccer at home or add much to any evening entertainment. On the other hand, it might be ideal for a picnic with small children.

If you feel disappointed that some features must be sacrificed to accommodate others—for example, if you have to give up the idea of a vegetable garden to accommodate the patio—then give the problem extra thought. One answer is to grow your vegetables in containers on the patio. They can be very attractive: some, such as herbs, will add fragrance, while Swiss chard is as colorful as many shrubs. Later, the need for the patio may diminish and you can remove it and go back to growing your own food.

# Structural components

## FLOWER BEDS

Wherever possible, incorporate beds of soil. The plants will be easier to manage, requiring less attention to watering and feeding than when grown in containers. Use topsoil that is guaranteed free of perennial weed roots.

In a traditional garden, the beds will need to be edged to define their shape and retain the soil. The edging may be of timber, bricks, tiles, or rounded stones. Where there is grass, edging the lawn every few weeks will maintain the shape of the bed.

By importing soil you can arrange to have alkaline or acidic conditions—or both, in separate beds.

## RAISED BEDS

Where the surface is solid, consider forming raised beds. There are many good reasons for doing this. Where there is no soil, such as in a rooftop garden, raised beds allow ornamental plants or vegetables to be grown. However, weight can be an issue (see page 40). In heavy, wet, clay soils which are difficult to garden, importing topsoil allows crops to be grown above the poor soil. Some plants prefer alkaline soil, while others demand acid conditions; with raised beds you can import whatever soil suits the plants you wish to grow. For those in wheelchairs or who find bending difficult, a raised bed can make the garden more accessible and easier to maintain.

Individual raised beds may be built for particular purposes. A small herb garden close to the kitchen will always be useful. It should be constructed in a warm, sunny position and filled with a free-draining, open, gritty mixture of soil without any manure. Try to avoid encouraging the herbs to grow strongly, as the flavor will not be as intense. A small Mediterranean-style garden with plants such as lavender, *Cistus* and *Aeonium* will require the same conditions. These plants dislike wet soil, preferring well-drained, impoverished ground.

## LAWN

It is difficult to justify including a lawn in a small-garden design. Good-quality green grass is at its best used as a foil to borders and beds of plants, with specimen trees dotted through it. There is the risk that a small patch of grass will be subject to hard wear and tear resulting in a worn, patchy, muddy surface.

There will be a lot of maintenance irrespective of size—with cutting, edging, weeding, feeding, and aerating all essential jobs. Where it is in shade, the grass sward will be thin, allowing moss to take over. There will need to be storage for the mower and somewhere to compost the grass clippings.

Having made my point, I acknowledge that there are undoubtedly lots of gardeners who love a lawn and are prepared to spend the time to have an immaculate green sward, regardless of size. So be it. If you allow your common sense to prevail, your lawn will not only work within the design but end up looking good.

Shape is important. The lawn needs to be brought into the overall design rather than appear the odd component.

Position it beside a hard standing area such as the patio and it will seem logical as another area to entertain or relax.

Where the mower has a roller, you will be able to have the wonderful light and dark green stripes. Mow the grass so that the lines run away from the house windows and patio seats. Looking along the lines will give the impression of a larger area of lawn.

Make grass-cutting easier by eliminating tight corners that are difficult to mow. Sweeping curves can be cut round with either a walk-behind or a ride-on machine. Where the grass comes up to a vertical object, such as a wall or fence, some mowers will leave a line of uncut grass. Remove a 4in-wide strip along the base of the wall and replace it with concrete or a row of bricks set flush with the lawn. This hard-surface mowing edge will accommodate the mower wheels, allowing all the grass to be cut.

Avoid planting tall-growing, floppy perennials and annuals close to the edge of the border where they will fall over on to the lawn and perhaps smother the grass.

It goes against the grain for me to suggest it, but as with the rooftop garden an artificial lawn may be the answer. (See page 46.) Just don't ask me over for afternoon tea!

ABOVE: *Curved edges to the lawn are so much more interesting than straight lines, and allow the path and borders to sweep round the grass.*
OPPOSITE: *A broad timber ledge to this raised bed allows you to sit and weed.*

## PATIO

Size matters—and while you really only need a patio large enough to accommodate a table and a few chairs, it would be nice if there could be sufficient space to entertain a few friends. Ideally, a space 12ft by 9ft will allow for this, with some furniture and perhaps a barbecue area. It is possible to buy kits in which the correct quantity and mix of tiles are pre-packed to provide a small circular patio area. Designing a gravel area or small lawn close to the patio will mean that your friends can spread out and circulate.

With some man-made block paving, the pieces are rumbled deliberately to chip the edges and give a mature 'been there for years' look. They should be laid on vibrated sand on a hardcore base without any gaps, which eliminates the need for grouting. Fine, dry sand needs to be brushed over the surface and vibrated into the cracks between the tiles. Other slabs should be laid with 3/8–5/8in gaps and grouted. Natural stone tiles are not uniformly thick and are therefore more difficult to lay. They are usually bedded on a mortar screed.

Cost of construction won't be cheap, the final bill depending on the price of the materials selected and the ease of access for excavation and bringing on site hardcore filling and materials. This is one operation that really needs to be carried out by professional contractors.

Bear in mind that where the surface is shaded it will become green with a film of algae. This may make the patio slippy, especially in winter. An annual clean-up with a power hose or treatment with a chemical algae-killer may become part of the maintenance regime.

Where there is enough space, dress the patio with containers planted with colorful and fragrant plants. Leave one portion of a hard-surface balcony or basement free of pots and plants, to allow a space where people can actually stand and have a conversation or cup of coffee.

## DECKING

Timber decking is particularly useful where the finished surface needs to be raised, or where a patio would require a consolidated, hardcore stone base but there is poor access for bulky materials such as hardcore and walling. It makes a lightweight, practical surface for a rooftop garden or balcony where there are load-bearing limitations that preclude the use of tiles or stone slabs.

Where I live, the rain is warm and soft but there is a lot of it. Wet timber is slippy. Over time, the wood becomes soggy, and the longer it remains wet the more likely one is to slip on it. In drier areas of the world, decking is a marvelous surface that lends itself to alfresco entertaining. The timber framework and piles, along with the decking, must be pressure treated with a preservative, and should have a guaranteed usable life of 15 years or more. Pressure-treated wood has undergone a process that forces the preserving chemicals deep into the grain. Hardwoods, such as beech and oak, will last longer than softwoods. When standing containers of plants on timber, use a saucer to prevent any soil-stained water that drains from the base of the container from marking the timber.

## GRAVEL

Some gravels are broken stone while others are rounded, worn smooth by river or sea. A grade of 3/8–½in is ideal for walking on, whereas ¾in and over is chunky and difficult to walk and stand on. You can buy every color imaginable, from white limestone and marble to buff, pink, fawn, brown, green, and even black. Mixtures with muted buff, brown, and fawn colors tend to blend well with plants and soil.

## ROOF-TERRACE SURFACES

Unless specified in advance, rooftop gardens will have a mundane surface to walk on. Subject to weight restrictions, one option is a thin layer of pea gravel with stepping-stone slabs. Alternatively, timber decking may be an option. Artificial turf may look green but it is plastic! Unless it is stuck to the roof surface it tends to turn up at the corners like a stale sandwich.

## PATHS

Even small gardens should have a "path" that directs you through. It may comprise stepping-stones spaced through the plants. The garden can be made to appear larger by means of a narrow strip of pathway that meanders around, doubling back on itself, enabling visitors to view the garden from a different angle while passing small plants and statuary that were previously hidden by larger shrubs.

Paths have to be practical. They should be firm under foot, with a non-slippy surface. In the small garden there is unlikely to be the space for a path wide enough to allow two people to walk side by side.

Gravel is acceptable, providing a pleasant crunchy sound which doubles as an intruder-deterrent at night. There will need to be timber or kerb edging on either side to retain the gravel.

Where there is an area of gravel, stepping-stones may be used to make a path through it. Space the slabs and try walking on them. Ideally they should be 12in apart. Any wider and you are goose stepping; any less and you have to take very small strides.

Paved paths are easy to walk on without the constant need to look where you are placing your feet. Low hedges of box or lavender to either side can be interesting, but tend to make the path look narrower.

The path may curve and meander in and out of planted areas, giving the impression of a larger garden. Where there is a traditional straight clothes line, the path needs to be straight and parallel to the line.

RIGHT: *An interesting hard surface, although it could be tricky for high heels!*
OPPOSITE, LEFT: *Where the patio is directly outside with easy access to the house, it becomes an outdoor room.*
OPPOSITE, MIDDLE: *Decking may be softened using plants and containers.*
OPPOSITE, RIGHT: *A gravel path can be edged by creeping plants.*

## CONTAINERS

Pots and containers are interesting and attractive in any garden—but essential where the whole garden comprises hard surfaces. Containers are available in all shapes and sizes, and in materials ranging from timber to stone, slate, earthenware, ceramic, plastic, wire mesh, and metal. They may be used for growing climbers against bare walls or for producing home-grown fruit, herbs, and vegetables. They are the answer when it comes to planting up a rooftop garden or a balcony. Patio and decking surfaces cry out for planted containers to help soften the area and to add interest and color.

Containers are invaluable in the small garden. They add height, interest and color while providing growing space on a hard-landscape area. Individual pots may please you, or you may prefer a collection of different-size pots with a range of plants.

Always make sure that there are adequate drainage holes in the base of the pot.

While traditional earthenware and ceramic pots are still popular, other materials, such as metal, resin, natural stone, and plastic, have come to the fore. Pot colors may be co-ordinated with the leaf or flower color.

Extremes of weather can play havoc with containers; small inner-city gardens are fortunate in being less prone to frost. Many earthenware pots are sold with a frost-proof guarantee, but few are fired to a sufficiently high temperature to withstand a serious drop during a cold winter's night. Fine cracks appear, and these hold water. As the water freezes, it expands; this results in larger cracks, and pieces start to flake off. Eventually the pot falls apart. At the other extreme, metal containers can—especially in summer—absorb the sun's rays, heating up and drying out the soil-mix and cooking the plant's roots.

Timber in the form of half- and quarter-barrels, complete with metal hoops, that at one time held port or whisky have a rural, almost country-cottage look. These hold enough soil-mix to grow larger specimen trees, shrubs and climbers. The formal, square, Versailles-type wooden container looks as though it was made for the patio, especially when planted with a standard specimen clipped bay tree.

You can achieve an interesting effect by planting small clipped box balls in tall, slim, metal containers. Where you are contemplating more than one, you could try varying the height of the containers and have a whole family of "things".

A word of caution. Alibaba-type containers, where the curved shoulders of the pot are wider than the neck, are a wonderful design and pleasant on the eye. However, if such a pot is to be planted, be sure to use annuals that are discarded at the end of the season. The shape is useless for long-life shrubs where plants are re-potted as they outgrow the pot. After a season, a plant's root-ball will be larger than the neck of the container. The only escape for the plant is for you to break the pot.

Hanging baskets and mangers work well on walls and railings where they add another level of color. Bear in mind that where they are to be watered and fed in situ the water will drain out of the base on to whatever is below.

LEFT: *Containers are available in all shapes and sizes but make sure there are drainage holes in the base.*

OPPOSITE: *Clay pots have more appeal than plastic.*

## PONDS AND WATER FEATURES

I believe that every garden, no matter how small, and every gardener, no matter how grand, will benefit from the sound and sight of running water. Even a small tinkling flow of water has a soothing sound. The rippling movement caused by a single drip or a volume of water flowing and tumbling over pebbles or rocks is magical, and never fails to hold a visitor's attention. A plant's perfect reflection on the surface of calm water or the mirror image broken by the vibrant flowers of water-lilies is possible with the smallest of ponds.

To hold the water you can use a fibreglass moulded tank, a liner, or, for very small features, a large waterproof bucket or barrel. Moving water relies on a pump, which needs electricity, so design in a waterproofed exterior power socket.

Where space is really tight, consider a water feature that is vertical and attached to a wall. The whole feature—including the sheet of water and the reservoir in the shape of a trough— may occupy a width of only 2ft.

A small stream can be designed to flow through an existing patio, taking up no additional space and adding interest and sound to the sitting area.

## ARBORS

In larger gardens there may be the space to have a secret garden, but with the small garden there simply isn't the scope to subdivide an already small plot. A small, enclosed arbor will serve to provide a quiet area for reflection, study, or to pass the time with a friend. The arbor is not very different from a pergola.

The construction may be timber or metal, with a floor of gravel or paving.

Often it will be more enclosed, with a solid back and sides, providing a private, secretive, "wrap-around" feeling. Usually an arbor is designed to seat two people, with the bench being part of the construction. Being smaller, it is more suited to the garden where space is at a premium. What makes it special and differentiates it from a bus shelter or a guard's hut will be the use of climbers and shrubs to clothe the sides and roof. Including plants with fragrant flowers and aromatic foliage will enhance its appeal. Where the arbor is at the far end of the garden, it is logical that the path should head in that direction.

ABOVE: *Water features can be accommodated in the smallest of gardens.*

## SCULPTURES

There is no garden too small for a piece of sculpture. Whether it be wood, stone, or bronze, providing it is suitably sized it will blend in, having that wow factor when discovered. A small figurine looks good on a plinth set into a clipped yew niche. Do make sure that it is firmly grounded and not likely to fall over and cause an accident. If it can be securely fixed, that may also prevent it from being stolen.

A sundial has its uses. Not only for telling the time, but as something to direct a path towards. Even those made of concrete and out of a mold lose their mass-produced look as they take on an overcoat of algae and lichen. A bird-bath has the same aesthetic function, but is also practical as a paddling pool for wildlife, allowing you to watch their ablutions.

Here I am going to annoy some gardeners. Please don't adopt a garden gnome! One is probably acceptable, but collecting them seems to become a habit—or else they breed! The best of them are garish and the worst are hideous. On the other hand, if you really want a gnome, make it obvious rather than concealing it to give a sudden shock as it leers out of foliage at your visitors.

ABOVE, LEFT: *A scented arbor with roses and honeysuckle.*
ABOVE, RIGHT: *Each to their own and this sculpture makes a statement.*

# Practical solutions to problems

## BASEMENT GARDENS

In basement areas a lack of access can make for difficulties. It can be very messy carrying soil, compost, plants, and hard-surface materials through the house. One solution is to lower the materials, and remove debris, by rope or winch over the surrounding street- or garden-level railings. Make sure you don't block the footpath or cause an obstruction to pedestrians.

A sheltered, sunny, south-facing wall gets the plants off to a good start. Free-draining, gritty soil that has been enriched with old, well-rotted manure will remain warm for longer than wet, heavy clay soil. White-painted walls, mirrors, and pale-colored reflective gravel mulches will help give the plants the impression they are in sunnier climes. You can buy a purpose-made reflective mulch of woven aluminium and polythene in the form of a mat. This suppresses weeds while allowing movement of water, nutrients, and air through to the soil, at the same time reflecting light back up into the plants.

### Dos and don'ts

— Do grow fragrant plants.
— Do paint the walls before planting.
— Do position pots of plants at the outside edge of steps.
— Don't use deep-rooted plants.
— Don't overfill containers with soil-mix.
— Don't use bulky growing shrubs.

## BACK YARDS

With luck, the concrete floor won't be thick, making its removal less difficult. You can rent an electric-powered jack hammer, but the broken concrete will still need to be removed—if you are lucky, there will be access for a wheelbarrow. As much of the work will need to be done by hand, consider the aching back and blisters before undertaking the job!

A simple operation is to paint the walls a brilliant white, using an exterior emulsion. It is amazing how much difference this makes, bouncing the available light off all the surfaces and dispelling the gloomy look.

### Dos and don'ts

— Do fix trellis to walls for plant support.
— Do check that imported topsoil is weed-free.
— Do raise the patio for more direct sun.
— Don't plant tall shrubs against the north-facing wall.
— Don't allow gutter drains to get blocked.
— Don't allow vigorous plants to grow over the walls into neighbors' plots.

## FRONT GARDENS

For the driveway, gravel will be softer-looking than tiles and less obnoxious than concrete, or asphalt. Gravel and porous man-made tiles also allow water to percolate through to the lower ground, avoiding run-off which—when swollen by lots of hard-surfaced front gardens—can lead to flooding. A few stepping-stones to either side of the parking bay will avoid the risk of damage to high heels on the gravel. Keep containers well back from the parking space, as a nudge or bump won't do the vehicle or the containers any good.

It is possible to have a lawn where a car is parked. Several products are on the market whereby a durable, tough plastic honeycomb is laid on a firm vibrated sub-base and the pockets filled with good-quality, stone-free, screened topsoil. The grass seed is sown in the usual way and, after germination, is cut, fed and watered as for a normal lawn. The honeycomb framework will support the weight of a vehicle and looks like a standard front-garden lawn.

### Dos and don'ts

— Do plant perfumed plants at the front door.
— Do screen the garden from the roadway.
— Do make the front-path surface interesting.
— Don't have a lawn unless it looks good.
— Don't allow tree roots to damage the garden.
— Don't plant solely deciduous plants.

## LONG NARROW GARDENS

Simple, relatively cheap make-overs are possible! One way is to gravel the whole of the surface with stepping-stone tiles laid on mortar through the gravel.

Where it is possible to excavate, the holes may be filled with good-quality topsoil and planted. Tall bamboos planted in pots will act as a screen while also providing movement and sound as the leaves are rustled by the breeze. Timber trellis will allow climbers planted in the ground or in containers to grow upwards, partially hiding any pipework to above eye level.

Alternatively, part of the alley may be covered with a timber pergola. The wall you own can be drilled to carry a horizontal timber beam 8–9ft above ground level. This will support one end of the horizontal overhead rafters. The other ends will rest on vertical posts

Climbers scrambling up and over the rafters can form a colorful walkway. Where the space has to accommodate garbage cans and bicycles, a trellis screen planted with climbers will make them less obvious.

### Dos and don'ts

— Do screen part of the garden.
— Do curve edges of borders.
— Do mix plants to have a patchwork of colors.
— Don't have high boundaries.
— Don't have your most noticeable planting at the far end of the garden.
— Don't design the path down the center.

## ROOFTOP GARDENS

Construction limitations and the physical delivery of materials must be considered, and follow-up and ongoing maintenance catered for.

Make sure there is easy access. You may be prepared to climb a ladder, but it is not going to be possible to manhandle many plants and materials the same way—and your friends and guests may not appreciate having to climb it!

It may be possible to winch materials up an outside wall, but that sort of operation is best left to a professional landscape contractor who will have valid insurance cover.

Ensuring safety requires you to take an even more active role when you are well above ground level. The complete perimeter must be made out of bounds, with railings or some other solid surround. It must be high enough to prevent an adult from leaning over and preferably without foot-holes that would permit children to climb on to it.

Weight is a limiting factor. Check with the builder the load-bearing qualities of the roof. If the building is old, seek the advice of a quantity surveyor. Use lightweight plastics or timber for the sides of raised beds. Avoid heavy ornamental containers. Soil-based mixes are heavier than soilless varieties but will require less watering. Ensure that the drainage holes in containers aren't blocked, as waterlogged mix will become heavy and the plants will suffer.

Plants will have to be grown in containers. These may include barrels, tubs, pots, and hanging baskets. Vegetables, fruit, and perimeter-screening plants may be grown in raised beds. Tiered staging may be used to enable additional pots of plants to be displayed, but make sure it is well secured, preferably backing on to a wall.

The floor of the roof garden will benefit from surfacing. Patio tiles may be too heavy, but timber decking might be an option for the sitting area, with a layer of 3/8–½in gravel denoting the pathways.

## Dos and don'ts

— Do concentrate on hardy evergreen plants.
— Do choose shrubs with small leaves that won't suffer in the wind.
— Do frame a good view with permanent plants.
— Don't use timber decking if it will always be wet and slippery.
— Don't use heavy railway sleepers for raised beds.
— Don't exceed the weight limits.

## BALCONY GARDENS

Many of the landscaping problems associated with rooftop gardens, such as weight limitations and work access, are common to balconies. Everything has to be transported through the house or apartment. There is no space to store even small tools such as secateurs and trowel. Fertilizers and pesticides all need to be stored inside the main building, as do cushions for outside furniture.

Where balconies face the afternoon sun, they can become very hot. An automatic drip feed and watering system can save time and prevent plant roots from drying out in your absence. Avoid the use of metal containers in full sun; the surface will heat up, drying out the soil mix and cooking the plant's roots.

### Dos and don'ts

- Do check the clips holding planted mangers on balcony railings.
- Do use interesting and non-slip floor tiles.
- Do have fragrant plants.
- Don't plant very vigorous plants.
- Don't plant spiny-leaved plants.
- Don't ignore evergreen plants for winter interest.

## PRIVACY AND SCREENING

Where space is at a premium, it is tempting to erect timber fencing to ensure shelter and privacy. This can be attractive, but requires regular treatment to preserve the wood and retain the color. The screen needs to be sufficiently high to do its job effectively, but apart from on the sunless side of the garden it would be a shame to block light and cause shade. Vertical board fences are strong, with the boards supported on horizontal timber rails bolted to concrete posts. The 6in-wide boards are spaced with ½in gaps between them, which removes any degree of privacy. They are ugly and unsuited to the small garden.

At design stage and thinking of plants, bear in mind that where there is room to plant, a living screen in the form of a hedge of flowering shrubs, leafy plants, or evergreen conifers is preferable to a solid wall or fence. Such hedges require ongoing maintenance of pruning and feeding, but they are living and become part of the garden, whereas fences and walls need to be painted and will always be lacking in character. The plants also have the ability to filter and slow down the wind, while a solid boundary forces the wind to come over the top causing turbulence in the garden. This will be at its worst at a distance two and a half times the height of the screen: wind blowing against a 6ft-high wall will produce turbulence 15ft in from the wall on the garden side.

Wooden trellis partitions, with trained shrubs or climbers, positioned between the patio and your neighbor may do both of you a favour. Timber trellis panels comprise thin laths of treated timber stapled to form a square or diamond lattice pattern. They make an attractive screen and are well suited to climbing plants. A sun bed may then be positioned to get maximum sunlight yet be invisible from the other side of the trellis. The height of boundary walls and fences can be increased with trellis bolted along the top. The boundary may be jointly owned, so consult your neighbor before undertaking to change the existing perimeter.

Lapboard panels are made of thin, wavy-edged horizontal boards overlapped within a timber frame. Woven and wattle panels have a short life and are quite flimsy; they are made from willow or hazel rods woven to form square panels.

Where the garden is overlooked from above by balconies and windows, or the basement garden is at the front and open to public scrutiny, "roofing" in part of the garden may be the answer. A small arbor or pergola covered with screening climbers will keep you safe from inquisitive eyes.

## STORAGE

One of the main complaints made by owners of small gardens is about where to store the essential tools. A wheelbarrow is a really useful piece of equipment but it has to be kept outside. There will have to be a store, albeit small, tucked out of sight and screened by plants; you should allow for this in your design. Small tools such as secateurs, pruning knife, and saw are easy to store, but since they are in constant use, leave them somewhere handy.

I have already mentioned that short- and long-term (winter) storage for the lawn mower may pose problems, but it is not just the mower. Some tools are essential, and while a plastic bucket may replace a wheelbarrow, you will need to have other tools such as spade, fork, rake (at least one type), trowel, and secateurs. A kneeling-pad is more than useful; it can make the difference between your weeding and not bothering to weed.

Small, lightweight, metal storage sheds that take up little space are available. These are not sheds you can go into; you have to stand outside and reach in. Most gardens can be designed to allow for a small space between the rear of a bed and the boundary; put your storage shed here, screen it well with evergreen shrubs and it will never be noticed. Store the garbage and recycling bins beside it with easy access to the rest of the garden. If there is some space left over, use it for a custom-made compost bin. That way you can put back some useful humus into the garden.

RIGHT: *This storage shed blends in with the surrounding plants and offers support to the clematis.*

OPPOSITE: *Virginia creeper works well in the summer and fall, but it will become see-through when the colorful leaves drop in winter.*

## CREATIVE CONCEALING

Where screening is required to hide a particular object, such as a compost heap, or bicycle stand, or to divide and enclose a secret garden, use plants rather than inert fences or walls that will require regular maintenance. Avoid planting very vigorous climbers such as the deciduous *Fallopia baldschuanica* (Russian vine) which will take over and smother all before it. A line of trained cordon apples or pears will provide cover in summer, adding interest with flowers and fruit. In winter their bare stems will help to break up and screen what is behind them. Bear in mind that with trained trees there is the additional maintenance work of pruning, training, and supporting the branches.

A flowering hedge, such as evergreen escallonia, will add color, while the year-round density of a formal clipped yew hedge will make whatever you are trying to conceal disappear. In the northern hemisphere, if the garden is in full sun, positioning a small tree to the south of the sitting area will provide privacy but also create shade. A dense twiggy tree, such as a birch, will result in deeper shade than a more openly branched crab apple or ornamental cherry tree.

Walls and fences can be unsightly, especially if they are in full view and facing important windows. Where plaster is flaking or cracks are appearing in stonework, you will need to have the construction checked by a qualified building surveyor. Assuming there is no serious fault, decide how best to rectify or camouflage the eyesore.

Evergreen plants will cover up unsightly surfaces, but be sure to select plants that will cling to or remain close to the upright. Bulky evergreens that want to lean away from the vertical will use up too much valuable space. In winter, deciduous shrubs and climbers such as roses, climbing hydrangea, and Virginia creeper have to rely on their tracery of bare branches to provide some screening.

Facing the offending fence or wall with timber lattice, woven hurdles or trellis panels will improve the outlook. Make sure these are firmly secured and that the wall will support their weight along with that of the plants. If the wall needs maintenance or regular painting, one possible solution is to hinge the panel to the wall along the base and attach the top of the panel to the wall with two or three hooks. That way, when necessary, the panel and its covering of climbers may be lowered to the ground and raised back to the vertical after the painting work is completed.

## MANHOLES

Manhole and inspection-chamber covers are eyesores. They cause frustration in that it seems they never need to be opened until the day after you cover them up. Camouflage them by standing containers of plants on top or mulching over the top with gravel. To find the concealed lid, stamp your feet: a dull noise will pinpoint its exact location. Where tiles, slabs, or block paving are being laid, use a recessed metal cover that accommodates a layer of tiles. The whole lid, tiles and all, is lifted for inspection. Only a thin band of the metal surround is visible.

RIGHT: *Being evergreen, escallonia makes an ideal flowering hedge.*
OPPOSITE: *A good crop of juicy pears may be grown on cordons trained on wires against a sunny wall.*

## CHANGES OF LEVEL

It is wonderful to be able to take advantage of a sloping garden. Where the slope is gradual, the whole garden can be made more interesting. Steps may be incorporated to accentuate changes in level. Taller plants may be grown at the lower level without looking out of proportion. An additional layer of low-growing, carpeting plants such as *Ajuga* (bugle), heathers or *Helianthemum* (rock rose) will disguise the sloping ground.

Where the slope is severe and at an angle exceeding 20 degrees, it may be necessary to terrace the garden or to build a retaining wall at the base of the slope and backfill with topsoil to reduce the gradient. Include in your design a slit plastic drainpipe, 3–4in in diameter, at the base of the slope behind the wall, to take water away and prevent it from building up and seeping through. This low wall may be finished with a flat coping, allowing it to be used as seating. The coping may be constructed of flat pieces of rock, reconstituted stone (concrete) or pressure-treated timber. A dry-stone wall may be used to give additional vertical planting space, for example with small alpines planted into it. These are best put in position as the wall is built, with the roots of each plant surrounded by a small pocket of soil. If the stone immediately above each plant is slightly sloped towards the rear, rain-water will run down towards the roots. Select choice alpines that are neither short-lived nor with an aggressive habit.

Another alternative is to make gabion walls. These are certainly different and, while I think the designer has to be careful not to let them become gimmicky, they are strong and easily built and can look colorful. To make one, pile or stack rocks, stones or pebbles into wire-mesh cages, then build these to the desired height. Use your imagination and select smooth, round river stones or broken sandstone with muted fall shades. Slate works well. There is also the opportunity to infill cracks and gaps between the filling with soil and plant alpines such as *Lewisia, Sedum* and *Saxifraga*.

Where an area for sitting has to be incorporated on sloping ground, it is easier to construct decking than a patio, for which retaining walls have to be built with a hardcore infill before the slabs or tiles may be laid. Decking can be raised on timber piles, allowing the ground to slope away below the deck. You can build steps from the lower level using lengths of timber decking; if there is more than a single step, construct a handrail. Where the ground falls away from the deck, play safe and form a balcony rail to prevent your guests from stepping off the edge of the deck.

## WORKING WITH WEIGHT RESTRICTIONS

Some aspects of gardening can be hard work, and lifting and moving heavy weights is seldom enjoyable. Where everything has to be carried down to the basement, up to a balcony garden, or right up to the roof level, any way of lightening the load is to be welcomed.

It is essential that you check with your builder, building control department, or local planning department for any weight restriction when landscaping on balconies or roof gardens. Unless the construction was designed to take the additional weight of containers, compost, plants, and materials, it is better not to add to the load.

Where there is some leeway in what can be added weight-wise, play safe and use soilless composts which, even when wet, are lighter than soil-based John Innes compost. Avoid solid, heavy stone tiles or gravel; instead use lightweight timber decking or lay artificial grass sheets.

## SOLUTIONS FOR LESS CAPABLE GARDENERS

Sometimes small gardens are more difficult to maintain than those with open spaces and more room to manoeuvre. Where the gardener has difficulty getting down and kneeling, simple jobs such as weeding, pruning, and even thinning out seedlings can be tricky.

For those working from a wheelchair, narrow paths and tight corners can be a nightmare to navigate. Smooth, level paths are easier than loose gravel to move along. Access needs to be ramped rather than stepped, and beds should be no wider than 4ft to allow plants in the center to be reached from either side.

Lifting the level of the soil by constructing raised beds makes weeding and pruning easier. It also allows the plants' attributes—especially the smell of flowers and foliage and the feel of particular leaves—to be appreciated.

Don't clutter up any open spaces such as the patio or decking with lots of containers. Position them along the walls or sides, leaving the main area clear for moving about.

RIGHT: *An unusual raised bed using wire gabions filled with builder's materials.*

# Chapter 4—
# Choosing plants

You will have your own reasons for having a garden and for the selection of plants in it. Many considerations will help to make a varied and enjoyable garden.

When you are selecting plants for a small garden, it is essential that they be worth their space. They need to perform well over as long a period as possible and either disappear below ground, as with perennials, or still be presentable during their off season. The collection needs to be made up of plants that will offer color and display throughout the four seasons. You will need to retain small gaps to allow for the spread of plants; these spaces may be temporarily filled either with bedding annuals, such as wallflowers, polyanthus, pansies, and busy Lizzies or with clumps of small bulbs, such as snowdrops, crocus, species tulips, and miniature daffodils.

# Plant selection

Just as small is beautiful when it comes to designing, with plants less is more. Packing plants into a given space is just about acceptable for a display garden at a show, but is disastrous if copied in your own patch. The individual habits of a plant need to be understood, otherwise the tall ones will hide the dwarf, compact varieties, and the vigorous will smother the slow-growing. In this respect, finding out the ultimate spread of every plant is every bit as important as knowing its ultimate height.

It is also worth remembering that although the garden is small, that doesn't imply that only small plants can be incorporated. A large specimen, such as the Japanese maple, *Acer palmatum*, may eventually become too large and out of proportion. At that stage it may have to be removed, but for at least a decade or two it will provide shape, texture, and color, allowing lots of smaller plants to be grown under its elegant canopy.

Where the garden is sheltered and sunny there is an excuse to try a few of the more exotic plants. Undoubtedly, we are all experiencing warmer, milder, seasonal weather, and, within the limits of your hardiness zone, there is the opportunity to grow a few plants normally associated with hot climates. These may range from olive trees to agave and protea; if they succumb to a late spring frost, replace them with something less adventurous.

As a precaution, mollycoddle half-hardy and tender plants. Wrap them in plastic bubble wrap or horticultural fleece from late fall through until late spring. Where they are growing in containers, use a gritty, free-draining soil-based mix. In fall, move them to a sheltered position protected from cold biting winds and wrap the container in bubble wrap. A high-potash feed in early fall will harden up the young growths, preparing the plant in case of a severe winter.

A tiny pond or man-made boggy area will support an amazing variety of moisture-loving plants, expanding the species and year-round interest.

Early-summer-flowering candelabra primulas (*Primula bulleyana*) will self-seed, adding more colors to the planting. Hostas will thrive in moist soil, and a single variegated plant will—if you can prevent slugs from attacking it—brighten up a dull, shaded corner. There is no law against mix and match: if there is the space, plant a cranberry among the ornamentals. Cranberry needs wet or swamp conditions to succeed; while providing you with fresh fruit it will also manage to look attractive with flower, fruit, and winter-leaf color.

A damp area will also encourage frogs to take up residence, and there is no better control of slugs than your own personal prince in disguise. Where there is shallow water, you can watch birds take their daily bath at the bottom of your garden.

## COLOR

First-time gardeners immediately think of color, and early plant selections are usually all summer-flowering. Do you want to have a color-coordinated garden where all the colors are in separate areas making up a pattern? There are gardens with long borders devoted solely to white flowers. Personally, I find the idea grand but the show monotonous. In the small garden it is perfectly feasible to have a small bed where all the plants flower at the same time and are a single color. However, out of season it will be disappointing.

On the other hand you could rainbow plant, with all the flower shades coming together in a riot of color. I have never worried about plant colors clashing. They might do on the catwalk or as wallpaper, but in the garden with lots of green foliage the colors will blend to make an effective, enjoyable display. Do whatever turns you on. It is possible to have too much color in a small space, but the problem would be the mass rather than the mix. Even then it would be a nice problem to sort out!

RIGHT: *Rainbow colors may look awful on wallpaper but in the garden they make a wondrous riot of color.*

OPPOSITE, LEFT: *Horticultural fleece may be used to protect tender plants from light frosts.*

OPPOSITE, RIGHT: *It's hard to beat a Japanese maple for spectacular fall color.*

## SHAPE

Plant shape can be important. Some gardeners prefer compact, rounded shrubs, such as *Skimmia japonica* 'Rubella', while others love the tall spires of delphiniums, *Verbascum* (mullein) and hollyhock. Architectural plants with big, hand-shaped leaves, such as *Fatsia japonica* (Japanese aralia) and the tall, sword-like leaves of *Phormium* (New Zealand flax) are eye-catching but can have only a limited life in the small garden before outgrowing their allotted space. Ground-hugging conifers and shrubs stay out of other plants' space yet add color at soil level.

If you have decided on some topiary in the form of standards, balls, pyramids, or spirals, they will need regular clipping to retain the shape, and feeding to ensure steady growth. Where they are being grown in containers, watering may be a daily task in summer.

TOP LEFT: *The big hand-like leaves of Fatsia japonica are impressive.*
TOP RIGHT: *Tall spires of hollyhocks lend a cottage-garden appearance.*
BOTTOM LEFT: *The sword-like leaves of Phormium have a tropical look.*
BOTTOM RIGHT: *Skimmia forms a rounded evergreen shrub.*

## TEXTURE

Texture is unbelievably important. I never go for a walk in my own garden—or any other garden—without unwittingly feeling leaves and the trunk of trees. Smooth and glossy (camellia), deep-veined (*Viburnum davidii*), velvety (*Hydrangea aspera* ssp. *sargentiana*), and softly hairy (*Stachys lanata*) are just some of the descriptions for the foliage of common plants that can be found in most gardens.

With some plants there is movement only when a gale is blowing. Others such as bamboo gently move in the slightest breeze making a soothing, whispering, and rustling sound.

TOP LEFT: *The deep-veined evergreen leaves of Viburnum davidii are highlighted by frost.*
TOP RIGHT: *Some hydrangeas have leaves that resemble velvet.*
BOTTOM LEFT: *The glossy evergreen leaves of camellia are complemented by perfectly shaped flowers.*
BOTTOM RIGHT: *The common name 'Lamb's ears' perfectly describes the softly hairy leaves of Stachys.*

# Types of plant

## BULBS, CORMS, AND TUBERS

Every garden should have clusters of bulbs appearing at intervals throughout the year. They are almost guaranteed to flower, and most of them will continue to do so year after year, multiplying over time. They take up very little space and have the added bonus of allowing other plants to cover the area when they are dormant.

A nice thing about gardening is that gardeners are always thinking ahead and planning for the future. There is no room for pessimism. Even in the middle of summer it is time to think of and plan for next year's spring color.

I have no intention here of constantly referring to "bulbs, corms, tubers, or rhizomes". While they are all different they are, with a few exceptions, planted in the same way. To avoid long-windedness I will usually refer to them as bulbs.

When buying, make sure the bulbs are from a reputable source and it states on the packaging that they have not been taken from the wild. The golden rule is to buy the best you can afford. Cheaper usually means smaller, and in some cheap packets the bulbs may not have sufficient food stored in them to allow them to flower the first year. Check that they look healthy with no damage and no signs of early growth starting. When buying loose bulbs, select the largest. Any that feel soft should be left in the store.

Bulk net bags of daffodil bulbs are often available at a cheap price. Make sure the bulbs are round in shape, ready to flower. Those that are flat on one side may not flower for at least one more year. It is difficult to examine them in the sealed bag, but with luck only a few will have damage. Some bulbs—such as hardy cyclamen, lilies and fritillaries—are sold individually; these can be expensive, but good-quality bulbs are well worth the extra cost.

Not all bulbs need to be planted as soon as they have been bought. Most spring-flowering species may be planted after the summer-bedding annuals have been removed in early October—but if you wait until then to buy, you can only have the best of what is left. Summer-flowering bulbs such as begonias, dahlias and gladioli will be on sale from late winter. Store them somewhere cool and dry—and please don't hide them away and then forget all about them until the next clear-out of the cupboard! Daffodils need to make roots before winter and should be planted at least 3 weeks before heavy frosts.

Bulb-planting is not complicated, but the better you prepare the soil, the better will be the results the following spring. Depending on the size of the bulb, space them 2–6in apart. The normal planting depth for bulbs is two and a half times the height of the bulb, so a small crocus ¾in high is planted about 2in deep, while a daffodil 2in high is planted about 5in deep.

There are some exceptions. With the long-stemmed tulip species, such as the Darwin types, planting them 8–10in deep will reduce the losses after the first year and the bulbs may be left in the ground.

The planting design is a personal thing. Some gardeners love to plant drifts and whole beds of not only the same species but also the same variety, making a massive single-color display. Others are more laid back and prefer to mix the colors and species, giving a rainbow effect.

Bulbs may be used to add interest to shrub and perennial beds that are without color at that time of year and might otherwise be left boring and dull. They are excellent as gap-fillers while you wait for the shrubs to spread and take up the allotted space. As a dot plant, a single tall lily, gladiolus, or tulip can lift the bed of annuals or low-growing perennials.

RIGHT: *Groupings of bulbs planted at a depth of two-and-a-half times their height will make a good spring, summer, or fall display.*

RIGHT: *Whether in the border or a window box, there is nothing to beat the scent and show of hyacinths.*
OPPOSITE: *Small flowering spring bulbs are cheap and easy to grow.*

## Best bulbs for small spaces

Lilies are a must. The scent of a group of three bulbs of *Lilium candidum* (Madonna lily) or *L. longiflorum* (Easter lily) will fill a small basement or balcony garden with perfume.

Then there are the hardy cyclamen, such as *Cyclamen coum* and *C. hederifolium,* with dainty pink, cerise, and white flowers in late fall and winter, and with marbled green-and-white patterned leaves to die for.

With the beautiful, summer-flowering bearded iris, the rhizome is like a big thick root. It should be planted in a sunny position with the rhizome laid horizontal just in the soil, with the upper side visible. It needs to be baked by the sun for a good show of flower.

Big, bold dahlias and gladioli may not be everyone's choice for the small garden, but they do produce a lot of color. There is one gladiolus I always find space for in any garden design: *Gladiolus callianthus,* sometimes labelled *Acidanthera bicolor* var. *murieliae.* It produces spikes of up to ten funnel-shaped, pure white flowers, each with a purple mark in the throat. The flowers are incredibly fragrant. Being slightly tender, it succeeds best when grown in pots of well-drained soil mix in full sun.

Where a few dwarf bulbs are tucked into a corner, or beyond a bend in the path as a clump in a border curve, they can, when suddenly come upon, create a pleasant surprise.

Small-flowering bulbs such as *Iris reticulata,* crocus, species tulips, and snowdrops are ideal for early color in the rock garden, in containers and window boxes and as a carpet under specimen ornamental and fruit trees grown in pots.

The heady scent of hyacinths,

lily-of-the-valley, and freesias will, in succession, add fragrance to the garden from spring until late summer. Where there is shade, the early woodland bulbs such as *Anemone blanda* (windflower) and *Eranthis hyemalis* (winter aconite) will flourish, dying down in early summer before the ground dries out.

Most small bulbs are excellent in containers on the patio and as a welcome either side of the front door. Hanging baskets are ideal for dwarf bulbs such as winter- and spring-flowering snowdrops, crocus, tulips, cyclamen, and hyacinths. Where winters are harsh, bulbs in containers may be killed if left above ground, as the soil chills to the outside temperature.

Snowdrops are best transplanted while still in leaf, but are seldom available at this stage. If purchased in the fall, soak the bulbs in water overnight before planting.

If you are making a wild flower garden, include some wild garlic, but plant it in a container to prevent it from spreading further than you wish.

Window boxes are tight for space, but will look good from inside with a double row of fragrant hyacinths or cyclamen.

Naturalizing bulbs in the lawn needs careful consideration. If the foliage is long or broad, as with daffodils, it won't have turned yellow and died down until 6–8 weeks after flowering. In the meantime the leaves mustn't be cut, or the goodness can't go back to bulk up the bulb for next year. The lawn will become an untidy mess with long straggly grass. By the time it can be cut, the base of the grass will be bleached, leaving the lawn pale for at least two cuts. Tall-flowering bulbs are best suited

to rough grass that may be left and cut in June. Smaller, early-flowering crocus are ideal for naturalizing in lawns as the thin, short leaves die down early in the grass-cutting season.

Mark where the bulbs are being planted using a cane or by spreading a layer of grit on the surface. It is easy to forget, come along before the end of the year, plant something in what looks like a gap and accidentally chop up and disturb the existing bulbs.

Squirrels, both tree and ground, are the real pests of bulbs as they dig them up. Birds love them too—but note that they have more of a liking for yellow-flowering crocus bulbs than purple, striped, or white. I have no idea how they know the difference when they are planted in the ground, but they do.

Mice will also do considerable damage. The best protection from all these "pests" is to cover the planted areas with fine wire mesh and let the bulbs grow through it.

## ANNUALS

An annual plant is one that germinates, flowers, sets seed, and dies in the one season. Not all bedding plants are annuals. Some—such as pelargoniums, polyanthus and pansies—are perennials that are grown as annuals and removed after flowering has finished.

For the last decade there has been a constant stream of new varieties of tried-and-tested annuals. Great improvements have been achieved, although not all new varieties have been better than those they aimed to replace.

Annuals are raised from seed. The seed may be sown early in seed mix and protected from frost in a greenhouse or garden frame, or inside the house on the windowsill.

Read the supplier's instructions on the seed packet. Larger seed is sown deeper than small seed. Very fine seed, such as begonia, should be sown on the surface of moist compost and left uncovered. Some seed needs daylight to germinate, while most prefers to be in the dark covered with newspaper.

Later in the season when all risk of frost is past, seed may be sown outside in rows for transplanting when sufficiently large, or sown thinly in well-raked fine soil where the plants

are to flower. Thin the seedlings, then allow them to grow on to flower. If the ground is prepared for sowing and then left for 7–10 days, any weeds that germinate can be removed just before the seed is sown, giving it a head start on the next batch of germinating weed seedlings.

Depending on the region, small plug plants may be available by mail order from nurseries that specialize in growing young plants individually in molded plastic trays.

Larger plants ready for planting out are available in garden centers and stores and at street markets.

Annuals are ideal for planting in containers, such as hanging baskets, mangers or large pots. Use multi-purpose soil mix. Make sure there are good drainage holes in the container, and don't fill right to the top: leaving a 2in gap between the top of the mix and the rim of the container will make watering easier. In the average store-bought soil mix, the nutrients will have been exhausted within 5–6 weeks, and thereafter constant watering and feeding will be necessary.

In the garden, cultivating the soil 8in deep will get the plants off to a good start. Nipping out the growing tip of most young annuals will encourage side-shoots to form, resulting

in a bushy plant with many more flowering stems. The plants should be spaced to cover the soil completely without becoming congested. Small annuals will be happy spaced 8–10in apart.

There is no end to the design possibilities with annuals. Color is important, and with these cheap plants it is possible to paint the small garden with vibrant shades of every color from purest white to deepest purple-black. Planting batches of the same variety will produce bold splashes of a single color. In the evening, a mass of white flowers can be startling. Some annuals such as the tobacco plant, *Nicotiana sylvestris,* exude their fragrance at night, while others, such as sweet peas, drench the surrounding area in scent during the day.

Well-behaved annual plants may be used to edge paths, while riotous nasturtiums will cover impoverished ground with rainbow colors. Informal planting schemes will form a colorful background without seeming too obtrusive. More formal schemes will create interest with the overall shape and pattern of colors.

Annuals may be cheap and cheerful, but as gap-fillers between expanding permanent plants they have no equal. From a spring sowing you will have a colorful patchwork in flower from early summer until late fall.

They may be used in hanging pouches, mangers, and hanging baskets to disguise unattractive walls, pipework, and railings. Many of the common annuals—such as pot marigold, aster, snapdragons, cornflower, and nemesia—are excellent as cut flowers, and a few planted in the perennial cutting border will extend those flowers available for the dining table.

ABOVE, LEFT: *Nasturtiums produce more flowers in poorly fertlized soil.*
ABOVE, RIGHT: *Remove spent sweet pea flowers before they start to seed.*
OPPOSITE, LEFT: *Individual bedding plants in styrofoam trays can be transplanted without suffering a setback.*
OPPOSITE, RIGHT: *Shake seed into the palm of your hand for controlled sowing.*

## PERENNIALS

Perennials are high-maintenance plants, but where the herbaceous perennial bed is planted in topsoil that is free of perennial weeds there will be less work. Weeding has to be done regularly, to prevent weeds such as buttercup or couch grass from getting into the clump and through the root area—where they become impossible to eradicate, resulting in your having to dump the whole clump. Most perennials are divided every 2–3 years, with the old center portion being discarded.

Taller-growing species, such as delphiniums, hollyhocks, and *Verbascum* (mullein), need some form of support to hold the flower stalks vertical and prevent the foliage from lying on other plants. These drawbacks aside, it's worth stating that in late spring, summer, and fall, a well-designed herbaceous perennial border is a thing of joy with a guaranteed wow factor.

If there is space to make the bed double-sided where it may be viewed from either side, plant taller plants along the center, with lower-flowering cultivars towards the front. When in flower, the bed will appear as a bank of color. If there is to be a border on either side of a path, consider designing the perennial planting to have a mirror effect, with exactly the same plants directly opposite each other in both beds.

Some gardeners advocate allowing the seed heads and dying leaves of perennials to remain throughout the winter as 'they look good outlined with frost and add interest to the winter garden'. Not for me; I think they look miserable and neglected. You risk encouraging plants, such as *Verbascum,* verbena, foxglove, and many others to self-seed, producing thousands of weed-like seedlings to torment you the following year. The dying and dead foliage also harbours slugs and snails. I will make a few exceptions: *Agapanthus, Dierama* and *Allium* seed heads are works of art and should be allowed to remain whether there is a frost or not.

## SHRUBS AND TREES

When designing for a small garden, be very careful with your selection of shrubs and trees. There are so many beautiful species, but unfortunately many of them will eventually outgrow their allotted space. Always make sure you get good information regarding height and spread of individual plants.

A shrub may be evergreen or deciduous and usually produces its framework of branches from ground level. Trees may also be deciduous or evergreen. Where there is space they are excellent for shelter and screening, but only a few are suited for small areas or for growing in containers. They can cause the rest of the garden to be in shade, which may or may not be welcome. When a tree is grown as a standard with a 6ft clear stem, other plants may be grown below the canopy.

Some plants are low-maintenance.

Shrubs such as camellia, *Pieris*, and *Kalmia*, for example, may never need to see a pair of secateurs. When they do, it is usually because they haven't been given enough space to spread out. Other shrubs, such as *Philadelphus, Weigela,* roses, and *Buddleja,* require pruning every year to encourage flowering wood and to keep the plant compact.

Would you like to grow a tree or two? Where there is a will, there will be a way, and having your own tree is possible in the smallest of gardens. There are trees that may be successfully grown in a large container, while others take up little space, having a columnar habit. The beautiful flowering cherry, *Prunus* 'Amanogawa', has stiff upright branches that allow the tree to remain slim without any midriff bulge. Trees, however small, provide shade, which for some plants such as woodlanders is essential. They are also good for berries, attractive bark, and fall leaf color.

If trees such as birch, cherry and *Acer* (maple) are to be included with bark in mind, be sure to keep their trunks clean. Green algae and dust disguise their beauty, yet just a few minutes a couple of times a year with a scrubbing brush and some tepid water will have the trunks gleaming and brightening the garden.

OPPOSITE, TOP: *Even after they've finished flowering, the seed heads of alliums add interest and color.*

OPPOSITE, BOTTOM: *It is a joy to walk between colorful banks of plants.*

ABOVE: *Providing the soil mix is acidic, camellias are ideal for pot culture.*

ABOVE: *Strategically placed evergreen plants will provide shelter and screening without blocking the view.*

## DECIDUOUS AND EVERGREEN

Deciduous plants lose their leaves in winter, while evergreens are just that: they are never without foliage. They do shed old leaves, but the plants remain well covered with younger leaves. Evergreens are particularly useful for providing shelter, filtering strong winds, and affording privacy. They will give shade all year. Many deciduous plants, especially trees and shrubs, provide excellent fall leaf color before the leaves drop. As these decompose they are the source of that lovely material leaf mould, sometimes referred to as "black gold".

Deciduous plants may be lifted and transplanted when they are leafless. Evergreens don't have a dormant period and are best moved or planted in late fall when the soil is still warm and rain is expected, or in early spring before their main growing period starts.

## QUICK-GROWING PLANTS

There are many reasons for wanting an instant garden; the in-laws dropping in early in the garden's life is as good a reason as any. Wanting to be able to enjoy your garden while you are still fit and active is not a bad reason either.

What you must avoid is planting the garden as if it were for short-term public display, with the plants packed close together for immediate effect. That is fine only at a garden show where, within a week, they are lifted out to be spaced properly back in the nursery.

Position the plants at the recommended spacing for optimum growth. Some shrubs, such as *Buddleja, Sambucus* (elder), and *Lavatera,* are very fast-growing and need to be spaced at least 9ft apart. Where you wish to cover the bare soil, infill between the permanent plants using annuals, biennials, or herbaceous perennials.

Large, container-grown specimen trees, conifers, and shrubs are available to give the garden an air of maturity. Make sure the plant is growing strongly and not stunted having become root-bound through being in the same pot for too long.

The use in a plant border of an individual plant (dot plant) that is different and larger than those surrounding it can be interesting, but in the small garden large dot plants can be overpowering, upsetting the balance and making the rest of the plants look pathetic. A single specimen tree or shrub will be expensive, but when positioned well can add to the interest and garden appeal. It might also impress the mother-in-law— especially if you leave the price label where it can be noted!

Bulbs are quick to flower and have few needs. There are species to give you color for most of the year, especially in late fall and winter when fewer other flowers are on display. Do label them in situ; it is so easy to forget where they are planted. This often results in their being dug up as you decide to plant something else to fill the "empty' space, or being walked on as they are appearing through the ground.

Annuals are also speedy little short-term plants. Sown as seed in spring, or bought as plants or small plugs in late spring, they quickly produce flowers and will be a riot of color from summer through to late fall. Plant them out when all risk of frost is past—densely so as to cover the ground and smother weed seedlings. Regularly deadhead the spent flowers to prevent them from wasting energy setting seed. Apply feeds of high-potash liquid fertilizer every 2–4 weeks. These plants will run out of steam in the fall or be killed by the first of the winter frosts.

Other shrubs, such as bush roses, and perennials such as *Doronicum,* will, if planted in late winter or early spring, flower the same year.

## PERMANENT PLANTING

With shrubs and trees you need to think long term. Some, such as lavender, are short-lived and generally, after 6–7 years they are past their best. Careful pruning and a suitable soil will extend their useful life. Others, such as rhododendrons, camellias, and yew trees, will easily outlive the person who planted them. They will reward good soil preparation before planting, and if they are fussy about the levels of alkalinity or acidity it will pay to provide the right conditions.

Incorporating some old, well-rotted farmyard manure in the planting pit and a handful of slow-release fertilizer will get plants off to a good start.

Sufficient space to grow sideways is important, long term, for the well-being of a plant and its neighbors.

In the small garden there is literally no room for mistakes; if a plant proves to be in the wrong position, remove it before it causes a problem. Find a good home for it elsewhere and fill the gap with something more suitable.

# Combining plants for year-round interest

One of the tricky aspects of plant design is guaranteeing year-round interest. You have to think beyond flowers and the seasons of flowering. Leaf color, texture, and shape play an important role, as does bark color, fruit, and berries. Plant shape and the outline of deciduous shrubs and trees can make a difference in winter.

There is no doubt that in a small garden the problem can be more critical. Every single plant must serve a purpose and earn its keep. The single-season flowering plant—such as hebe or hypericum—that becomes large may not be worth the space it takes up when it could be replaced with a collection of small gems—such as rhododendron, lavender, dwarf bulbs and centaurea—that collectively provide a show all year round.

Positioning the plants is important. Try to plant with the four seasons in mind rather than setting all the spring-flowering plants together and the other seasons' plants in their own groups. Slip in a few little extras where they are least expected. A cluster of pure white, new-year snowdrops pushing through a group of heathers long after their fall display has finished will bring cheer to a bed of plants that have hibernated.

Underplanting to form layers of color is a useful way of maximizing available space and creating year-round interest and color. 3ft-high mini-standards of lavender, willow, cotoneaster and *Euonymus* (spindle tree) may be underplanted with low-growing heathers and periwinkle. Upright conifers, such as the golden Irish yew, won't mind dwarf spring-flowering bulbs around their feet. Bare-legged climbing roses can be improved by underplanting with evergreen *Sarcococca confusa* (Christmas box). Not only will the bare stems disappear, but the winter fragrance from the lower shrub will be as good as a well-perfumed summer-flowering rose.

It is worth considering mix and match where, instead of being planted as a collection in a herbaceous border, the perennials are dotted through a mixture of shrubs. They are less noticeable in their off season and are supported by the nearby shrubs.

Evergreen plants will give year-round interest, whereas spring- and summer-flowering deciduous shrubs will have a bare framework of branches in winter. Where plants are being grown for shelter or privacy, choose carefully, selecting those that are well-behaved. Avoid species that tend to spread outwards thus taking up valuable space. Some climbers, such as *Clematis montana* and *Clematis armandii* 'Apple Blossom', are undoubtedly too vigorous for a small garden; they may scamper about with stems as long as 30–35ft.

Think carefully about where you site roses. They are colorful for 5–6 months of the year, but they really need companions if the bed is to look good all year. As they are thorny, don't site them too close to paths. Where climbers and rambling roses are used to cover arches and pergolas, the shoots will need to be trained and tied in to prevent accidents.

## LEAVES AND BERRIES FOR COLOR, SHAPE, AND TEXTURE

Sometimes there is one particular part of a plant that draws your attention and makes you want to own it. It could be the big, bold leaf shape of *Fatsia japonica* (Japanese aralia) or the filigree pattern of a fern. The feel of the leaf can be very sensual, with the bristly, hairy, upper leaf surface of *Hydrangea sargentiana* rasping like stubble on a chin.

Berries always work for me. The clusters of metallic-blue, ovoid fruit of *Viburnum davidii* never cease to amaze me – they must surely have been sprayed in a car factory.

A special group of plants for the small garden are those that provide interest all year round, combining plant and leaf shape with leaf, flower, bark, and fruit color to give best value for money and earn their keep in the garden.

ABOVE: *The metallic berries of Viburnum davidii add color to the winter garden.*

OPPOSITE: *Where space is at a premium, it is possible to plant layers with the taller plants growing out of the ground cover.*

## What and where to grow for leaf shape

— Bergenia 'Baby Doll': Large, glossy, mid-green leaves. Moist, well-drained soil. Full sun or shade.

— Carex elata 'Aurea': Arching, narrow, golden foliage with a thin, green stripe. Keeps its color well in summer. Moist soil. Sun to part shade.

— Geranium maderense: Deeply lobed, bright green foliage. Well-drained soil. Frost-free. Full sun.

— Phormium 'Sundowner': Sword-like leaves. Well-drained soil. Full sun.

— Rodgersia pinnata 'Superba': Large, deeply lobed, glossy, dark green leaves. Humus-rich, moist soil. Full sun or light shade.

— Yucca filamentosa 'Bright Edge': Lance-like stiff green leaves with bright yellow margins. Well-drained sandy soil. Full sun.

TOP: *The chestnut-like leaves of Rodgersia make a bold show from spring to fall.*
BOTTOM: *The spiky, variegated leaves of Yucca raise the temperature on a patio.*

## What and where to grow for berries

— Arbutus unedo 'Elfin King': Bright red, warty, strawberry-like fruit. Well-drained soil. Sheltered from cold winds in full sun.

— Callicarpa bodinieri var. giraldii 'Profusion': Metallic-like, dark violet berries. Fertile, well-drained soil in full sun.

— Gaultheria procumbens: Aromatic, deep red berries. Moist, acid soil. Shade.

— Ophiopogon planiscapus 'Nigrescens': Blue-black berries. Fertile, well-drained, acid soil. Full sun or light shade.

— Skimmia japonica 'Fructu Albo': White berries. Humus-rich, well-drained soil. Shade.

— Sorbus reducta: Crimson berries turning white. Humus-rich, well-drained soil. Sun or light shade.

TOP: *Callicarpa bodinieri var. giraldii 'Profusion' produces small pink flowers in summer followed by small violet berries in winter.*

BOTTOM: *Sorbus reducta forms a thicket growing 3–5ft high.*

## What and where to grow for texture

—Hydrangea sargentiana: Deciduous with stout bristly shoots and leaves. Blue-purple fertile flowers surrounded by white, sterile flowers in late summer. Humus-rich, well-drained, moist fertile soil in sun or light shade.

—Stachys byzantina 'Big Ears': Grayish-white, felted, mid-green leaves, soft and silky to the touch. Well-drained, fertile soil in full sun.

—Sedum spectabile 'Brilliant': Gray-green, smooth, succulent, toothed deciduous leaves. Deep pink flowers in late summer loved by bees and butterflies. Well-drained, neutral-to-alkaline soil in full sun.

—Viburnum rhytidophyllum: Deeply veined, glossy, dark evergreen leaves 8in long. Well-drained, moist soil in full sun or light shade.

—Paulownia tomentosa: Forms a large tree, but if coppiced in spring will make 6–9ft of growth in a season, with 12–15in-wide, bright, light green, deciduous leaves, hairy on the upper surface and very hairy on the underside. Well-drained soil in full sun and sheltered from cold winds.

—Verbascum bombyciferum: White, woolly basal leaves and white, silky-hairy stems. Alkaline, well-drained, impoverished soil in full sun.

TOP: *Stachys*. BOTTOM: *Hydrangea sargentiana*. OPPOSITE, TOP: *Sarcococca hookeriana var. humilis*. OPPOSITE, BOTTOM: *Cotoneaster*.

## What and where to grow for year-round color

— Amelanchier laevis: Young deciduous leaves bronze, then mid-green in summer, turning red or deep orange in fall. The pendant racemes of small white flowers appear in early spring, followed by edible, sweet, blue-black fruit. Well-drained, moist, acid soil in full sun or light shade.

— Sarcococca hookeriana var. humilis: Glossy, dark evergreen leaves. Clusters of small, very fragrant, pink-tinged white flowers, followed by small, spherical, blue-black fruit. Humus-rich, moist, well-drained soil in full sun or light shade.

— Mahonia aquifolium 'Orange Flame': Pinnate, dark glossy evergreen leaves, rust-orange when young and turning deep red in winter. The fragrant, yellow flowers appear in spring, followed by blue-black berries. Moist, well-drained, fertile soil in full sun or light shade.

— Corylus avallana 'Contorta': Mid-green deciduous leaves turning buttery yellow in fall on manically twisted stems, with pendant yellow catkins in winter and edible nuts in late fall. Fertile, well-drained soil in full sun.

— Cotoneaster 'Hybridus Pendulus': Small, dark evergreen leaves and small white flowers in summer, followed by bright red fruit in fall. Usually grown as a standard with the branches weeping. Well-drained, fertile, alkaline soil in full sun.

# Aiming for fragrance

Fragrance is one area where a small garden often scores. With large gardens it is possible to have areas where the fragrance of nearby plants is pronounced, but in the small garden the whole thing can become a perfume factory. The air can be filled with fragrance—and at all times of the year. My favorite time is winter, when the sweet perfume of flowering shrubs, such as *Sarcococca, Hamamelis,* and *Chimonanthus* is so noticeable on a cold, calm day. In summer, the scent of roses, *Philadelphus,* and lilies can almost be overpowering, while herbs, such as lavender, sage, and thyme, add to the aroma.

Cultivating fragrance is not so effective in rooftop gardens where there is considerable air movement that dilutes and removes the heady perfume. Conversely, fragrance in the basement garden can be overpowering.

There are some flowers that are definitely perfumed but you have to bury your nose in them to get the smell. Many roses are miserable in that respect; you can walk through a whole field of them without noticing any fragrance. Choose your varieties of rose carefully, making sure that they really do have good scent rather than just the hint of something pleasant.

Other flowers are more generous, allowing their scent to travel away from the plant and fill the surrounding air. The white winter flowers of the evergreen shrub *Sarcococca confusa* are tiny, yet the sweet fragrance is noticeable from a distance of 12–15ft. A single sprig of flower can fill a room with perfume.

Outdoors, perfume will be more noticeable on a calm day. In summer, the warmth of the sun will bring out the smells and allow the volatile oils of aromatic-leaved plants, such as lavender, to be released. In winter, on a calm day or in a sheltered corner plants' aromas will be more noticeable thanks to an absence of others such as those of newly-cut grass or barbecue cooking.

Position aromatic plants where they will be most noticed, for example close to opening windows, beside sitting areas and in containers. Fragrant plants growing overhead, for instance on a pergola, will drizzle their scent down. Rows of lavender edging a path may result in clothing brushing against the foliage and becoming impregnated with the delicious scent.

The flowers of some plants, such as night scented stock and evening primrose, remain closed during the day and then open in the evening to fill the air with a heady scent.

ABOVE: *Being surrounded by aromatic foliage and perfumed flowers is like sitting in potpourri!*

## What and where to grow for fragrance

— Daphne mezereum: Late-winter flowering. Moist, well-drained soil. Light shade.

— Lavandula stoechas (French lavender): Summer flowering. Well-drained soil in full sun.

— Mahonia repens 'Rotundifolia': Late-spring flowering. Well-drained soil. Deep shade.

— Philadelphus 'Lemoinei': Summer flowering. Well-drained soil. Full sun or light shade.

— Sarcococca hookeriana var. humilis (sweet box): Winter flowering. Humus-rich soil in shade.

— Syringa patula 'Miss Kim': Spring flowering. Well-drained soil. Full sun.

TOP: *Sarcococca hookeriana var. humilis (sweet box) dishes out incredible fragrance in the dead of winter.* BOTTOM: *French lavender loves well-drained soil in full sun.*

# Cutting border

The term "cutting border" sounds grand and like something that takes up a lot of space, and where there is plenty of room in the rural garden it is a most useful feature. In small gardens, the space devoted to flowers for cutting will not be generous, but a cutting border is still worth fitting into the design.

Try to design the bed to fit somewhere where it is not in full view. The idea is that using flowers from a separate source means the main garden display is not denuded to supply the indoor rooms. If you can tuck it alongside the vegetable or fruit garden, or to the rear of a shrub border or screening hedge, it will be less obvious.

With careful selection of plants, you can have flower and decorative foliage all year. There can be two or even three tiers of planting. The flowers of low-growing plants, such as primroses, polyanthus, and dwarf spring bulbs, make wonderful compact table displays during winter and early spring. Flower Carpet varieties of rose will produce blooms for seven or eight months of the year and often up to Christmas. Gladioli and lilies may be planted to grow up through the lower plants. A single tuber of a decorative or pompom dahlia will provide flowers from summer until the first frost. Taller, summer-flowering *Philadelphus* (mock orange) and bare-stemmed, winter-flowering *Hamamelis* (witch hazel) are both fragrant.

By cutting the flower spikes of delphiniums and lupins for use in the house you will encourage the side-shoots to flower a few weeks later. The stems will be shorter but still useful for cutting. Bedding plants, such as 'Ostrich Plume' asters, stock, cornflower, sweet pea, and marigolds, make wonderful cutting flowers. They are cut-and-come-again plants, and a few will provide cut flowers throughout summer and into fall.

# Avoiding poisonous plants and garden thugs!

Some dangerous plants are best left off the list. It is not unreasonable to plant foxgloves, despite the fact that the flowers and leaves are toxic. On the other hand, better safe than sorry. Children are unlikely to eat foxgloves, but most gardeners wouldn't feel as content planting any of the female yews, such as *Taxus baccata* 'Fastigiata Aurea', with its attractive, poisonous red berries. Poisonous plants with large berries, fruit, or seed are only for gardens where there are no children. Plants that irritate and blister skin, such euphorbia with its poisonous milky white sap, should also be treated with caution.

Then there are all those plants that are garden thugs. You buy them as attractive shrubs or perennials, plant them with tender loving care and they repay you by proceeding to take over the garden, spreading rapidly and smothering all in their path. Some of the ground-covering lamiums such as *L. galeobdolon* come into this category, along with the beautiful *Rubus cockburnianus,* with its pure white blooms covering dangerously spiny stems. In winter, after leaf fall, the bare stems are truly magnificent, but unfortunately this plant is a rampant spreader with vicious thorns.

Left: *Removing a few stems of Polyanthus and a bunch of daffodils would leave gaps in the display, but when taken from a cutting border they will not be missed.*

# Selecting plants that will be ideal for your garden

## BACK YARD

The résumé for plants for the back yard should include "ideally suited to growing long term in a container against a wall". If plants are tolerant of cool, shady conditions they deserve brownie points. Very vigorous climbers are to be avoided, as the walls will probably be short and little more than 6ft high. A lack of daylight and direct sunlight will mean that shade-loving plants, such as hostas, camellias, and spring bulbs, should be on your list.

ABOVE, LEFT: *In a sheltered basement garden it is possible to produce fruit on a loquat. It will be too large for a tiny garden but the leathery, corrugated leaves are attractive.*
ABOVE, RIGHT: *Where space is limited in a front garden, plants may be grown vertically on walls.*
OPPOSITE: *There is still space for plants in a small, low-maintenance back yard. Hostas love a dark, shady corner.*

## BASEMENT GARDEN

There are excellent plants that will tolerate the conditions of the basement garden. The secret of success is to prevent wall plants and climbers—such as clematis, roses, and jasmine—from scrambling for the light with all the flowers at the top and leaving you looking at bare-legged plants. Using evergreen shrubs with variegated foliage will ensure that the garden is alive throughout the year. With these as the bones or framework, you can build on the basic design, bringing in seasonal flower color.

Inner-city basement gardens are often totally frost-free, allowing all sorts of tender plants to be grown. *Opuntia cacti,* succulent *Agave,* king *Protea,* and subtropical *Grevillea* along with fruiting trees of olive, avocado, passion fruit, loquat, and pomegranate have all managed to thrive in inner-city basement gardens in New York, Denver, St. Louis, and other cities.

## FRONT GARDEN

Evergreen- and deciduous-flowering plants not only enhance the main entrance, creating a good impression on visitors, but also help to screen the car if it is off road and parked on the drive. Irrespective of size, a well-designed and well-planted front garden will be noticed by passers-by who have no other interest in the property.

Tall, columnar, evergreen plants, such as *Juniperus scopulorum* 'Skyrocket', will screen and soften the view of the house. Where the garden is really small, with the front railings or fence only a few feet from the front window, it is preferable that passers-by become interested in the garden rather than looking through your windows. A gravel area with a single specimen dwarf *Acer palmatum* (Japanese maple) underplanted with hardy winter-flowering cyclamen should do the trick.

A typical chocolate-box-picture cottage garden is another option, where a riot of seasonal color is crammed into the space. Plants should include climbing roses with hollyhocks, wallflowers, columbine, pelargoniums, daffodils, and sedums.

## LONG, NARROW GARDEN

It is both desirable and possible to make a long, thin plot look less narrow. Plant a few bulky evergreen shrubs, such as *Elaeagnus pungens* 'Maculata' and *Mahonia* x *media* 'Charity' that can be maintained by pruning at 6ft high, with a 3–6ft spread along each side, at a wide spacing and not opposite one another. As you walk through the garden you see it section by section, with the length disguised by these side baffles which give the impression of a series of small square or rectangle plots.

Plant something eye-catching with bold leaves such as *Yucca gloriosa* (Spanish dagger) halfway down rather than at the far end. A piece of well-shaped yew topiary will do as well.

## ROOFTOP GARDEN

For a rooftop garden to be a success there has to be a lot of detailed design work. Careful selection of suitable plants that will be tolerant of the climatic conditions and their exposed surroundings while still serving their purpose will be critical.

Taking account of the wind will be a priority. Make sure you appreciate the conditions at their worst rather than on a sunny summer's day. Some parts of the garden will be worse, owing to the tunnelling effect caused by wind being forced between walls and higher structures. There are tough plants, such as bamboo, holly, and evergreen oak, that will help to filter the wind. Perimeter see-through, laminated-glass screens can be attached to the coping on the top of walls to offer some protection when people are sitting down.

Unless shelter is exceptional, the main use of the rooftop garden will be in summer and fall, so you may want to select plants that are at their best during those seasons. Where the garden is in view all year round, a succession of color and interest will be needed.

In exposed sites you may need to plant short-lived and low-growing perennials and annuals that can be discarded and replaced before they suffer and become bedraggled.

Climbers will have to withstand considerable buffeting from winds. Twining plants, such as wisteria and honeysuckle, will get off to a better start than those such as ivy and *Hydrangea petiolaris* that support themselves with aerial roots that need time to adhere to the surface. Climbers, such as roses, will require constant tying in; use soft string that won't cut into the stems. Vigorous climbing clematis, such as *C. montana* and the evergreen *C. armandii,* should be avoided as, over time, they build up such a "sail" of foliage and stems that they will blow off their support or pull it down. From ground level, plants look good trailing over the side of the rooftop garden, but they need to be tough to withstand being buffeted and blown sideways.

A permanent irrigation system supplying water and liquid fertilizer to plant containers will save hours of watering and ensure that plants don't suffer when you are away on holiday.

With rooftop gardens there is always a movement of air, and newly planted material will suffer from transpiration until the roots become established and start taking up water. In the short term, until the plants become acclimatized, raise the humidity by misting the foliage and protect them from the wind by wrapping them in horticultural fleece.

ABOVE: *It is narrow, but plants in containers make this space look wider, and weaving around the plant foliage takes your attention.*
OPPOSITE: *The safety barrier in this rooftop garden is ideal for a scrambling honeysuckle.*

## STEPS

It all depends on the width of the access. If the steps are sufficiently wide, small pots and containers may be placed on one or both sides of each one. Where the steps turn a corner, the landing area will afford more space for a larger pot or a collection of smaller containers. It is important that containers should not impede access or block a way that may be a fire exit.

A railing will allow you to suspend hanging baskets brim full of annuals or Lilliputian vegetables or strawberries. Well-behaved annual climbers, such as *Thunbergia alata* (black-eyed Susan) and *Cobaea scandens* (cup-and-saucer plant), will scramble up and over handrails and railings. Plants may be changed with the seasons, with pansies, polyanthus, hellebores, and small bulbs making a show in winter, followed by wallflower and then the summer show of annuals. Night scented stock will bid your evening visitors welcome. Some candles or solar lights will set the scene for a pleasant evening.

Where the steps are against a blank wall, you might fix—above head height—mangers, hanging flower pouches, and hanging baskets to the wall and fill them with flowers, fruit, or vegetables. Plants that trail, such as ivies, nasturtiums, and lobelia, can make a show cascading down a plain wall.

Where steps are in full sun and sheltered from cold winds, in cities, tender half-hardy plants such as *Clivia* and *Strelitzia reginae* (bird of paradise) may be tried. Or, where the wind blasts right up the flight of steps, this may be a cold, inhospitable spot suitable only for hardy plants, such as *Ledum groenlandicum* and heathers.

## WORKING WITH SHADE

More often than not it is not the shade itself that causes problems in the garden; there are lots of plants that love shady conditions. Rather, it is what is causing the shade. Where large trees are providing the shade, the ground beneath the leaf-and-branch canopy will be dry and full of tree roots. These will have exhausted the ground of available nutrients. Evergreen trees will form dense shade all year and prevent winter rain from falling on the soil.

The north side of houses in the northern hemisphere is not only shaded but cold. Often cold blasts of wind are directed around the building, adding to the already miserable conditions.

Where the garden is a basement, the whole garden may be sunless with poor light conditions. In such a situation the plants may become spindly and drawn, stretching upwards towards the light. However, it is still possible to have a colorful and interesting small shady garden.

Wherever possible, try to improve the light conditions; partial or light shade is easier to cope with than deep shade. In the case of a shady basement or back-yard garden, painting the surrounding walls white will improve things by reflecting the light back on to the plants. Use exterior emulsion paint and carry out the work before planting.

Mulching with a light-colored or white gravel will again reflect light. Securing a mirror on a wall that gets the sun will bounce the bright light on to the shaded walls.

Improving the drainage by adding coarse grit will open up and lighten the soil, making it warm up more readily. A free-draining soil will retain heat for

longer, and where there is partial shade the stored heat will encourage growth.

Tree roots in the shade of the tree make planting difficult. Where the tree is large and mature, cutting a few small roots to form a planting pit won't do the tree any harm. With some trees, such as ornamental cherries and birch, there is a mass of surface roots. One solution is to top-dress the area with 1–4in of good topsoil and plant into that. Never exceed this depth, as many trees dislike their roots being buried deeper than normal. Keep the soil layer back from the vicinity of the tree trunk. Eventually some roots will rise up into the new soil, but by then the plants will be established.

Select the plants with shade in mind. Avoid Mediterranean-type plants with gray or silver foliage, as their leaves are coated with hairs to withstand strong sunlight.

Some shade-loving shrubs, such as *Acer shirasawanum* 'Aureum', have bright yellow leaves that are easily scorched

brown by sunlight. Lots of plants are true woodlanders, enjoying partial shade. Copses and woods are home to camellias, rhododendrons, honeysuckle (wild woodbine), and hostas. Ivies do well in shade, as does the golden hop (*Humulus lupulus* 'Aureus').

If you have dry soil in shade, plant the incredibly fragrant *Convallaria majalis* (lily-of-the-valley). Lots of the winter and early-spring bulbs, such as the snowdrop (*Galanthus nivalis*), winter aconite (*Eranthis* x *tubergenii*), hardy cyclamen (*Cyclamen coum*), and the windflower (*Anemone blanda*), have flowered and died down before the deciduous tree leaf canopy appears and the soil dries out. Winter chill doesn't cause them any concern.

ABOVE, LEFT: *The golden-leafed hop succeeds in light shade but is very vigorous.*
ABOVE, RIGHT: *Variegated lily-of-the-valley.*
OPPOSITE: *A well-used vertical space that is both ornamental and provides a supply of herbs.*

## WORKING WITH BRIGHT SUN

As gardeners, we are always wishing. Those of you who garden in full sun probably, at times, wish for an area of shade where you and your plants could chill out.

Mediterranean plants, such as *Cistus* (sun rose) and lavender love the sun and will happily grow in ground that has been baked dry. When herbs are grown in a sunny position, their flavor and aroma are greatly improved.

Other plants suffer in the sun, with leaves becoming scorched and flower colors fading.

Support wires for climbers growing on walls will heat up in the sun and can scorch the stems and tendrils of plants. Using plastic-coated, galvanized wire eliminates the risk.

The soil at the base of walls facing the sun is notoriously dry. Any roof overhang means that rain seldom lands at the base, so the soil heats up, causing plants left to fend for themselves to wither and possibly to die. Shrubs suitable for hot dry walls are available: *Ceanothus, Callistemon* (bottlebrush), *Cytisus battandieri*, and *Solanum crispum* 'Glasnevin' will enjoy and thrive in these conditions.

Soil will heat up where there is strong midday sun coupled with a lack of rain. Some plants, such as roses, dislike these conditions, preferring a moist, heavy loam soil sufficiently deep for the roots to go down at least 12–15in. Clematis prefer their roots to be cool while the foliage and flowers bask in full sun. Adding well-rotted manure to the soil will make it moisture-retentive. A deep mulch of gravel, slate, or bark applied when the soil is moist will help deter weeds and, more importantly, prevent moisture from evaporating.

ABOVE: *Bottlebrush and lavender love a hot, dry summer.*
OPPOSITE: *Vinca (periwinkle) is as tough as an old boot.*

## WORKING WITH THE WIND

"The North wind doth blow and we shall have snow" begins a children's nursery rhyme with a red-breasted robin as the central character. Along with the poor robin, plants growing in the northern hemisphere don't like the cold winter blasts from the frozen north. Unlike the robin, they can't tuck their heads under their wings—but they can be offered protection. Winter winds are often sufficiently cold to kill plants that are less than hardy. The east wind in spring is cold and will burn young foliage. Where gardens are close to the coast, salt-laden winds may cause serious scorch damage to evergreen plants and to the new growths of trees and shrubs.

Strong gusts of wind can be as damaging as gales, causing branches to break and uprooting young and old trees. Broken branches spoil a plant's overall shape, and the wounds are prone to fungal diseases such as canker.

Newly transplanted plants are very susceptible to the drying effect of the wind. Even a warm breeze will cause leaves to transpire, losing moisture that can't be replaced until the roots settle into the new soil and start taking up water. Keeping the foliage moist will reduce transpiration.

Rooftop gardens and open balconies are particularly prone to the effects of wind exposure. Only tough, hardy plants can tolerate the conditions, and even these, where possible, should be given some protection during winter. The wind effect can be exaggerated where it is funnelled between two buildings to emerge in the garden with extreme turbulence. Courtyard, back-yard, and basement gardens fare better when sheltered from direct blasts of cold air.

Make sure that pots and containers are secure and those with tall, leafy plants, such as bamboo, are prevented from blowing over in the wind. Wherever possible use a soil-based mix which, while heavier than soilless, is better for holding the pot in place. In late fall move planted containers that are not needed for interest or color to a more sheltered part of the garden.

In exposed gardens make use of some of the more common hardy, low-growing, and carpeting plants, such as alpines and dwarf bulbs, and ground cover, such as cotoneaster, *Ajuga* (bugle), *Vinca* (periwinkle), and some of the mat-forming junipers. Buy plants that are small rather than large, and avoid big specimen conifers. A small plant is easier to overwinter for the first couple of seasons, and thereafter better able to withstand the cold and the wind's buffeting. Treat with care shrubs and trees that have brittle, easily broken branches, such as *Cotinus* (smoke bush) and magnolia.

Where support is required, use a wooden stake or strong bamboo to grow the plant up. To avoid damaging the roots, insert the stake in the ground before planting. Use a rubber cushioning pad and strong, woven strap to hold the plant in place. Satisfy yourself that the tie isn't constricting the stem and cutting into the bark: check the plants at least twice a year, in spring and again in early fall.

Where necessary and if there is space, plant a boundary screen of plants to filter and slow down the wind. Plants in the ground will have to take their chance with bitter cold winds, but you can provide some winter protection from the worst of the elements. Form a wigwam around each plant using three or four canes pushed into the ground and tied together at the top. Cover this with fine plastic mesh or horticultural fleece to block the wind. Leave the top open to prevent the plant from becoming mollycoddled.

Small perennials that start growing early in the year can be covered in early winter with chopped-up straw, bracken, or leaves, held in place with netting or empty hanging baskets inverted over the loose material.

## CLIMBERS AND LIVING SCREENS

In small gardens, effective screening becomes a trade-off against available space. Many good evergreen shrubs have a habit of growing outwards as well as upwards, becoming bulky and using up valuable space. Careful selection for columnar conifers may solve the problem. Effective screening can become a disaster, throwing most of the garden into shade.

Wherever possible, try to plant a living screen that will filter the wind and look attractive in leaf and flower. Providing they are kept clipped, some evergreen hedges, such as *Taxus* (yew) and *Lonicera nitida* (shrubby honeysuckle) may be restricted to 12in in width. Bamboo is effective as a living screen, but will, in time, spread beyond its allotted space. Climbers such as the evergreen honeysuckle, *Lonicera henryi,* may be used to camouflage timber fences. Some climbers, such as wisteria, will need to be held in place with wires. With lattice fences the shoots can scramble through and remain in place without additional support.

## POLLUTED AREAS

If you live in a city or town, a perimeter living screen will considerably enhance the air quality in the garden. After a shower of rain, the leaves are brighter and cleaner with the layer of dust particles washed off.

Where pollution is severe, plants with leathery or glossy leaves, such as *Aucuba, Osmanthus,* camellia, holly, and skimmia, will be less affected than hairy-leaved plants such as *Paulownia.* A dense yew hedge is ideal for lowering the volume of roadside noise and filtering polluted air.

ABOVE, LEFT: *Tropaeolum peregrinum (canary creeper) is a tender annual climber that will grow to 9ft.*
ABOVE, RIGHT: *Skimmia and Osmanthus will tolerate dust, making them ideal for basement gardens.*

LEFT: *Bamboo makes a great living screen, but it needs to be restricted to prevent it spreading.*

83

## FRUIT AND VEGETABLE PRODUCTION

When the garden is small, and ornamental plants, the hard-surface patio, paths, and edible crops are all fighting for a share of the limited space, it is usually the vegetables that lose out. That is a shame because, undoubtedly, home-grown produce has a better flavor than store-bought. There is also an enormous satisfaction to be had from growing some of your own food.

The small garden throws up two problems for the gardener who is serious about home-grown fruit and vegetables. First, there is never enough space that can be spared for the many possible food crops. Then there is the problem of overall appearance in the garden. While in late spring the growing area can look pristine, with row upon row of young salads and transplants, by summer it is looking less formal and a bit untidy. By fall it can be a disaster, with bits and pieces of edibles remaining along with stumps and crops gone to seed, and the later crops of leeks, sprouts, and broccoli still waiting to be harvested. The fact that the growing plot needs to be in a sunny position doesn't help its case when that is the preferred spot for sunbathing and a glass of wine.

There are several options, all of which mean restricting the amount of crops that may be grown. Some vegetables are sufficiently ornamental to be grown in a bed of mixed shrubs and herbaceous perennials. Globe artichoke is a bold, architectural plant with large, deeply-cut, gray-green leaves. It will, by the third year, become huge, with enormous leaves. The secret is to remove suckers each spring and grow them on. That way the plant remains small but with fewer flowers. If the young buds are not harvested they open into large, thistle-like bright blue flowers.

Runner beans may be grown up obelisks where their red, white, or pink flowers add to the summer color. Jerusalem artichokes are grown for their tasty, knobbly tubers. Fast-growing, with the leafy stems making 9–12ft of growth by summer, they can form an effective screen around the sitting area. Swiss chard produces leaves with bright yellow, white, or red mid-ribs.

Giant wooden wine or whisky barrels with the tops removed, filled with soil-based mix and with holes cut in the side 15–20in apart, are ideal for a crop of strawberries. The fruit will be mud-free, but a net will be essential to prevent birds from clearing the ripening crop. Over the top of the barrel it is difficult to keep the net high enough to stop the birds pilfering. Here, instead of strawberry plants, sow or plant scallions and lettuce in the compost: you will have extra food for free and the birds will leave the vegetables alone. Bear in mind any weight restrictions before positioning a large barrel of soil mix on a balcony or rooftop. For the last word in barrel growing, fit the base with castor wheels similar to those on the bottom of boards used to move heavy pots. That way the barrel is easily turned to allow all the strawberries to receive equal amounts of sunlight.

The smallest of balconies will cope with a few hanging baskets or mangers attached to the railing. Where weight is a concern, use a lightweight soilless mix and plant tumbler tomatoes, strawberries, dwarf peas, onions, chives, herbs, lettuce, or any other dwarf vegetables that take your fancy. The crop won't be large, but you will have grown it, it will be fresh, and I bet you it will have a better taste than you could ever have imagined.

Top Left: *Globe artichoke is at home in the vegetable plot or the perennial border.*
Top Right: *Strawberries in hanging baskets are safe from slugs.*
Bottom Left: *Vegetables such as chard thrive in raised beds.*
Bottom Right: *A compact but productive plot that includes runner beans on obelisks.*

## Vegetables for the small plot
These may be divided into six groups:

— Salads, such as lettuce and scallions.
— Herbs, including the various mints and thyme, parsley, sage, and fennel.
— Root crops, such as carrots, potatoes, and parsnips, are invaluable in the kitchen.
— Greens, such as cabbage, cauliflower, and broccoli, are best fresh from the garden.
— Legumes, such as the different peas and beans, that tend to grow upwards and need support. Lastly there are my favorites, the posh vegetables. In this group I think of asparagus, artichoke—both globe and Jerusalem—and the sugar and asparagus peas.

— Then there those that are commonly grown but don't fit into these groups: tomatoes, both regular and cherry; green, red, and hot peppers; bush or climbing cucumbers; and even one of the miniature pumpkins or melons.

Whatever space can be designed in and set aside for vegetable-growing, it will be insufficient to grow all these crops. Bear in mind that some of the greens, such as cabbage, take up a lot of space. When considering potatoes as a crop, concentrate on the varieties that crop early; then even a couple of meals of your own tasty spuds will make all your efforts worthwhile. Main-crop potatoes to see you through the winter will take up too much space. It is possible to double-crop by sowing rows of scallions, radish, or early carrots between rows of lettuce.

Raised beds are ideal for the smaller vegetables, such as salad crops and herbs. Where space is at a premium, large containers, window boxes, and hanging baskets may be used for lettuce, small fruiting tomatoes, and parsley.

Some vegetables, such as brassicas, prefer an alkaline soil. The roots of crops, such as carrots and parsnips, will split if there is an excess of nitrogen fertilizer, and become distorted if grown in stony soil.

Peas and beans need support and tend to cast a shade over nearby crops.

For the best flavor, herbs will need to be grown in a sunny position, preferably in a gritty, free-draining soil. A few, such as thyme, sage, basil, and marjoram, won't look out of place in an ornamental Mediterranean shrub bed.

RIGHT: *In the small garden, interplant shrubs and perennials with herbs.*
FAR RIGHT: *Herbs in containers prefer a free-draining soil.*
OPPOSITE: *A wide selection of beans, rootcrops, salads, and soup vegetables can be grown in a raised bed.*

## Fitting in some fruit

If you are going to grow edible crops, fruit—in my view—has to be top of the list. Fruits taste so much better when they are picked fresh from the garden still warm from the sun. It is amazing how many different fruits may be accommodated in a small garden.

First there are the bush fruit. Even a single bush of gooseberry or black-, red-, or white currant planted in a mixed bed of shrubs will yield enough fresh fruit for dessert, tart, or even a pot of jam.

Cranberries and blueberries love acid soil that is constantly wet, and may be grown in pits in the open ground, lined with polythene to retain moisture. Alternatively, plant them in containers of an acidic soil mix in which the drainage holes have been blocked.

When fruit is planted in rows in the northern hemisphere, rows running north-south will get the maximum sun: in the east side of the row in the morning, as near overhead as it is going to get in the afternoon, and along the west-facing side in late afternoon and evening. This is particularly important for rows of tall-growing plants, such as raspberries. These should be planted on the eastern side of the plot, allowing lower-growing fruit (such as strawberries) and vegetables to be clear of the raspberries' shade by late morning.

Soft fruit, such as strawberries, may be grown in hanging baskets and mangers. Summer- and fall-fruiting raspberries produce their berries on tall canes. You can plant 5–7 canes in a 2ft-diameter circle in a shrub bed, with the canes tied at the top to form a pyramid or cone. The following year, the new canes are tied in to replace the previous stems.

Most fruit trees are too large for the small garden. An apple scion grafted on to a dwarf rootstock may allow you to have a single tree, but most varieties need to be pollinated by another variety.

There are small trees that may be grown in pots, but the quantity of fruit is obviously limited. Training the trees as espaliers—horizontal, cordon, or fan-shaped—against a wall will allow you to grow apple, pear, cherry, peach, or nectarine, but probably you will run out of wall space before you have planted one of each.

Shrub beds can be edged with horizontally trained apple trees. These do require summer and winter pruning, but one or two plants won't take up much time. They have two branches trained in opposite directions, parallel to the ground and at a height of 12–18in. If there is a sunny wall, plant it with cordon, fan or horizontal espaliered fruit trees. Choose from apple, pear, cherry, peach, or fig. In the northern hemisphere, the best position is against a sheltered, sunny, south- or west-facing wall. Where a patio or decking runs up to the wall, cut out a 12in x 18in planting hole. Make sure the soil at the base of the wall doesn't dry out. Dig in lots of old, well-rotted farmyard manure.

Fruiting vines may be trained over trellis or a pergola to provide fruit in late fall, as well as shade from the large leaves which will take on fall color. Like vegetables, fruit will best succeed in an open, sheltered, sunny position.

LEFT: *One gooseberry bush will supply sufficient fruit for my favorite dessert, gooseberry fool.*
OPPOSITE: *Private and sheltered, this pergola even offers fresh grapes overhead.*

# Chapter 5— Designing

When you are working with a small area, it is important that the finer aspects of design are not left out. The big vista and parkland are not possible but, by using plants to provide movement, color, shape, and texture, you can achieve a lot. Providing there are sufficient points of interest to keep your eyes moving around the landscape, the garden can seem larger. Mixtures of different flower colors at all times of the year are particularly useful. A small plant covered in flower, such as the compact-growing, yellow-flowering Rhododendron 'Princess Anne', or with interesting foliage, such as hosta, will be as eye-catching as a large tree or shrub. Larger dot plants in a planted bed give the impression of a bigger area.

# Tips and tricks

It is wrong to assume that lots of small objects, be they pots or plants, suit a small garden. They spell clutter and make the area appear even smaller. Restrict the number of objects, make them large and reduce the range of plants with tiny leaves. Lots of specimens of a single plant planted in groups and bold clumps will give an impression of space.

The fewer different surfaces the better, if you want to make the garden look larger. Positioning something at the far end to catch people's attention will give the impression that the garden is longer than it really is. A small tree or an interesting figurine can work well. Select a tree that will provide interest over a long period with, say, its bark color, fall leaf color, and fruit or berries. Trees with different shapes, such as weeping and columnar, will draw your eyes to them.

Usually, small gardens are bounded by the straight lines of buildings, walls, and fences; therefore, wherever possible, design patios and paths to have curves. Planted areas with sweeping edges to the borders will compensate for the straight boundaries and, at the same time, eliminate corners in the lawn that are especially troublesome and difficult to mow.

Light and shade in the garden will help to give the appearance of a larger area. Where the shadow of a plant falls on a vertical surface, from some angles the image is doubled in size. If the branches and foliage blow and sway in the wind, that movement is accentuated by the shadows dancing in time with the plant. When part of the garden is in shadow and the rest is in full sun, the shaded part looks like a separate area divorced from the brightly-lit part.

Above, Left: *You can't help but wonder where this slate path is going as it disappears round the bend.*
Above, Right: *A partially concealed object "discovered" among the plants.*

# Entrance

First impressions do count. Whether you are approaching the garden through the front gate, via patio doors from the interior, or down steep steps directly off the street, it is important that there is sufficient design input immediately on view to create a wow factor. It is also important that the whole garden cannot be seen with one glance, but your eyes are drawn past the nearest plants to a more distant object. Having enough room for at least two people to stand together looking at the garden will, in itself, suggest plenty of space. If the entrance path or set of steps finishes at the patio or deck, that will allow you to stand and let your visitors get their first look at the garden.

The design should allow for hidden corners containing choice plants, sculpture, or seating. Suddenly coming across such an area leads one to believe that the overall garden is larger than it really is. A trickling water feature that can be heard but not seen will intrigue and heighten curiosity. And where it is in shade, it will suggest that the immediately surrounding area has a lower temperature.

Fragrant plants at the entrance bid your visitors welcome. Where it is possible to enter through an arch planted with perfumed flowering climbers, or with matching container-grown aromatic plants flanking the way, sweet-scented memories will be cherished long after the visit.

TOP: *A secret part of the garden dropped into the middle of a planted area.*

ABOVE, LEFT: *Flowering plants such as wisteria at the front door are the best way to make visitors feel welcome.*

ABOVE, RIGHT: *A path leading to a hidden seat which draws your eye to the more distant part of the garden.*

# Linking in with out

Where the garden is viewed through patio doors or low windows, you can make the garden appear larger by bringing some plants indoors. Yucca, lilies, and azaleas will all give the impression of being part of the garden, extending the view from the indoor plants to the far end. Where the windows are higher, plant up window boxes with seasonal plants to provide color and interest all year round.

It is crucial that where the garden is immediately outside patio doors or French windows, and can be seen from a main living room or bedroom, it looks interesting and colorful—but, more importantly, inviting.

There needs to be a path, stepping-stones or a patio to start you on your journey, and please don't have the whole garden immediately on display. It may be small but, like a lady's, some of its attributes are best experienced and appreciated over time. The path should disappear at some point. Even if it only curves behind a shrub, it suggests there might be lots more to see beyond the obvious. As with the entrance, perfumed plants close to the patio or alongside the path will be an enticement to explore your garden.

Surprise yourself. Small groupings of dwarf spring bulbs tucked in behind other shrubs mean that, someday, you will head out to the garden and... there they will be in all their glory. You may be pleased, proud, excited, or downright delighted; whatever your reaction, that is what gardening is all about.

Interesting vegetables, such as Swiss chard with its red, yellow, or white

rhubarb-like stalks, can create interest when planted through annual bedding or a herbaceous perennial border. Until they are harvested they add bright color to the bed. The giant perennial globe artichoke is well suited to temporarily filling a gap between plants in the shrub border, where its enormous, deeply divided, gray-green leaves are architectural and its enormous edible flower buds open into big, blue, thistle-like flowers. As the other shrubs spread sideways and meet, the artichoke may be sacrificed or moved to another planting position.

Try to bring the path around and through the garden. If it can be designed to meander, the garden will have a larger feel. Approaching the same plant from a different direction can make it look like a different plant altogether. Returning to the house entrance at a slightly different angle will leave visiting gardeners thinking that they have been on a longer walk than the garden actually permits.

A cold, wet morning may not be the best day for working in the garden or showing it off to visitors, but if there is color and interest you can admire the view from indoors in the warm.

ABOVE, LEFT: *Stepping-stones disappear to encourage investigation.*

ABOVE, RIGHT: *Swiss chard is colorful as well as edible, so use in the perennial border.*

OPPOSITE: *In gardens where the weather is uncertain it is essential to have the "outdoor room" accessible to the house.*

# Vertical planting

Use all the available space. Don't forget your vertical surfaces. Walls, fences and trellis can be used to support shrubs, climbers, and fruit, often doubling the growing space without making the garden look smaller. There are three main groups of climbing plant, categorized according to their manner of growth. The first type are those plants with aerial roots, such as ivy, and those with sticky tendril tips, such as the Virginia creeper. These are self-clinging and do not require any additional support when grown on walls or trees. Then there are the climbers with twining stems, such as honeysuckle, wisteria, and clematis, with their curling petioles. Where the surface is solid, as with a wall, these climbers will require additional support. The third group are the shrubs with hooked thorns, such as climbing roses, with the ability to hold on to tree trunks and trellis.

All climbing plants will benefit from support when they are newly planted, to encourage them to become attached to the vertical surface. Twiggy branches of birch will help to retain the stems in contact with the support until they become attached. Sticky tape will hold them in place until they can manage to cling on and start climbing. Where there is only hard surface and no soil, holes may be excavated and filled with topsoil or compost. Alternatively the plants may be grown in containers.

LEFT: *Training rose stems around an upright will encourage side shoots that will all produce flowers.*

# Lighting

Lights dotted through the garden are magical. The clever positioning of outside lights will make the small garden appear much bigger. Spotlit moving water falling from a fountain or tumbling over rock is something I never tire of watching. Areas in deep shade can be brought to life with a few lights. A walk in the garden at dusk with lights to define and light a winding path can be truly romantic.

Design the position of each light with care rather than flooding the whole garden like a sports stadium! Spotlighting a single plant in the garden tends to make it look larger. With darkness between you and the plant, the distance to the plant seems to be greater. A plant's shadows make it look larger. Not only will spotlighting plants positioned in front of a wall provide shadows, but the shadows of those such as bamboo will seem to dance in the slightest breeze.

Highlight single plants, such as a small, winter-flowering shrub or a tree with good-colored bark. Experiment with the plants you choose to highlight. Some, such as rhododendron and some *Astilbe* varieties, can look washed out when lit at night. Others fold up their petals, opening their flowers only during the day. Uplighting a tall, columnar tree lifts it out of the darkness and gives the impression of additional height. Watching the moving shadows cast on a white wall by a single light playing on bare branches and leaves can be almost hypnotic.

Small, diffused lights may be used to outline the path and patio area. A row of small lights along one side of a pathway not only makes night patrols and romantic walks safer but gives the impression of a much longer path.

If you are in doubt regarding the type of lights and the lighting plan, seek the advice of a lighting expert. The system must be installed by a qualified electrician. Consider adding a few extra outdoor, waterproof power points for electrical equipment, such as barbecue, power tools, and water features.

Electric cables will need to be buried; always insist on armored cable that won't be damaged by contact with a spade or digging fork. To save wasting time they should be laid in trenches at the start of the landscaping and before other hard- and soft-landscape work begins.

A cheap but effective system of low-density lighting can be had with solar lights. There are no cables or power supply, and they are without risk. Their effect at night depends on the hours of sunlight during the day, the power generated being stored in each individual battery. Obviously they are more effective during summer, but they will continue to produce a glow even in winter. Some are very stylish, with light that changes color.

ABOVE: *Highlight individual plants after dark—just make sure the plant is worthy of the candle!*

# Trompe l'oeil

If you want to impress your visitors, construct a trompe l'oeil. This trick of the eye appears to show an open door or lattice-work leading to another space or garden. It is, in fact, an image painted on a blank wall or framework attached to a solid wall, often with a mirror as the "opening" and reflecting what is in the existing garden. It is very clever on two counts: your visitors believe what they see, and when the trick is pointed out to them they are amazed and impressed. Personally, if I wanted a trompe l'oeil I would employ an artist or carpenter to ensure it really worked.

# Awning

A triangular sail of creamy white linen, cotton, or canvas held aloft on timber poles and straining wires, almost horizontal to the ground, conjures up the impression of hot, balmy days with azure-blue, cloudless skies. It offers protection from the sun, providing a well-lit but shady area. Unfortunately, such weather conditions may not always prevail, but even if the sky is lumpy and leaden, the awning will deflect rain. It gives the screening and privacy so desirable when neighbors' windows and balconies overlook your garden. Parasols and table umbrellas are of limited use—but they do set the scene for afternoon drinks in your outdoor room.

# Outdoor bar

The outdoor drinks bar is becoming as popular as the barbecue and is the ideal companion to it. It may be used for soft drinks at children's parties or for aperitifs before dinner. Power for a small fridge or cooler will allow chilled drinks to be served. Subtle touches include the use of wine corks to mulch nearby plant containers. You can start hoarding your own or come to an arrangement with your local bar or restaurant. Inserting wine bottles upside-down in concrete to form the bar floor is eye-catching and different from a tiled surface. The bases of bottles are strong, and providing only the bottom is exposed they will withstand reasonable wear and tear. You may consider using plastic, non-breakable glasses that won't come to or cause harm when set down in odd corners of the garden.

LEFT: *Murals and trompe loeils can be quite subtle and this one has the virtue of making the space feel more enclosed.*
OPPOSITE: *A garden bench must not only look inviting but be comfortable too.*

# Garden furniture

Don't buy the first set of outdoor furniture you see in the garden center or store. Look around. There are some wonderful traditional hardwood sets that are as comfortable as those in your dining room. Perhaps you want something more modern in brushed steel, wrought iron, alloy, or plastic. The choice is personal, but I will give you a few thoughts.

Make sure your purchase is not too big to be carried out through the existing door to the garden, and that there is space for it in the garden. Think of the man-hours needed to maintain timber by oiling and staining, or for the painting of metal. Consider storage. Perhaps what you are buying is weather-proof and can be left outside all winter (probably under a waterproof cover). Uneven patio surfaces can be a nuisance, causing furniture to be unstable and rock about.

Another alternative is to use built-in furniture, where tops of dwarf walls are used for seats and a slab of natural rock or slate jutting out from the wall becomes a table-top—rather like a kitchen breakfast bar. Lengths of tree trunk can be carved into seats, but these are usually too heavy and awkward to move about. Cushions that can be brought indoors at the end of the day make for a comfortable rest.

The barbecue can be a permanent feature, built of local stone or brick. Finding the right site for a free-standing barbecue can be tricky. It may have to remain outside all year under a waterproof, protective cover. It is best kept away from overhanging plants as the heat may scorch their foliage or cause fire. Try not to annoy neighbors by allowing smoke or the smell of food to invade their privacy. Positioning a barbecue on gravel rather than on a tiled patio will prevent greasy food stains from marking the surface.

Children's play equipment may be needed, and both this and the garden furniture could eat into the area ideally to be devoted to plants—but a clever designer can double up. Low-growing herbs may be grown under the bench and between cracks in the patio. The framework of a swing makes ideal support for fragrant sweet pea, charming black-eyed Susan, tasty runner beans and other annual climbers. Alpines in pots can adorn the table until it is needed for food and drink.

ABOVE: *Dressing up your garden for a party can be as simple as stringing up some colorful paper lanterns.*

# Festive dressing-up

It is good to be able to use the garden throughout the year. In winter, in many regions of the country, there are times when it is enjoyable to sit out in the weak early afternoon sun. Even when the weather drives you indoors, it is gratifying to look out at colored lights with shadows playing in the garden.

Wherever possible, try to include in your design a tall shrub or small tree that can be seen from the windows. It will make an excellent framework for strings of small outside lights. Where there is a waterproof power point in the garden, installation is simple. Most such lights work through a small black transformer box which may be sealed in a polythene bag and tucked out of sight.

I am not of the opinion that colored lights are for use only over the Christmas period. They look good all year round, and in the late evening in summer they are magical. Where they are an almost permanent feature, make sure they are securely fixed. Hold them in place using string that is soft, to prevent the expanding stems from being strangled. Where the supporting tree or shrub requires pruning, remove the lights before starting work.

Paper lanterns, outdoor candles, and wind-operated colored fans will help to create an atmosphere conducive to relaxing and a party mood.

Hiding Easter eggs in the garden is fun for both children and adults—and any that are missed become the property of the gardener!

Birthday garden parties can be as formal as one wishes: you may opt for cushioned seats, canopies, wine, and soft music or, on the other hand, for ice cream, streamers, and pop.

# Common sense

I have already said that designing a garden requires a modicum of common sense. It would be daft to position a small greenhouse in a shaded area or where there is a frost pocket. Similarly, a site where the ground slopes will be fraught with the problems of leveling both inside and outside the greenhouse. You don't need to be a qualified designer to know that a position in full sun and sheltered from cold winds is the ideal place for the greenhouse.

The surface of water is always level, so trying to make a pond on ground that slopes makes for a lot of hassle. You have to dig out and mound the ground to make it level, otherwise the water will be overflowing on one side and only halfway up the other side of the pond. Building a pond away from the sun in partial shade will reduce the risk of green water and algae which seem to thrive in direct sunlight.

The vegetable and fruit garden should be in a sunny position. It deserves to be where the soil is at its best without risk of drying out or becoming waterlogged. It will also benefit from being screened by a hedge. In winter the plot can look untidy with bits of crop still to be cleared or harvested.

If you are going to have a fruit cage it must be made to look neat and professional, otherwise it will stand out like a sore thumb. A sheltered, sunny site away from overhanging trees is desirable. Where there are only a few trees or fruit bushes, it may be simpler to cover individual plants with a fine plastic net to prevent bird damage.

It makes sense to position fragrant flowering plants close to opening windows and in containers on the patio where their perfume can be appreciated. Where there is a garden seat against a wall or under a small tree, plant a perfumed climber that will grow up and drizzle down scent as you relax.

# Bringing it all together— your final design

This is the point where lots of new gardeners convince themselves that the design discipline is best left to the professional garden or landscape designer.

Not so. A dollop of common sense mixed with some knowledge of plants and you are on your way. You have a big advantage over the professional designer: you know the type of garden you want to achieve.

It is desirable not only that, through design, your garden becomes personalized, but also that the finished garden lives up to your expectations. Some so-called garden designers will try to draw up a plan that they like themselves. Don't accept it. It is your garden, not theirs. In order to avoid confusion and argument, list your requirements and preferences at the start. This will also be a check-list for those who are designing their own garden.

One of the trickiest aspects of garden design is fitting as much of your wish list as possible into the space available. This can't be hit or miss. It would be a shame to squeeze the patio until it became so small as to be useless. Planting a rampant climber such as the vigorous rambling rose 'Kiftsgate' where there is only a 6–9ft run available will result in tears and a badly mangled rose.

Once you have listed all the features you have decided on, you need to draw your plan on paper to make sure that collectively your ideas fit the space. First of all, take site measurements. Make sure these are accurate. Get a friend to hold

the other end of the tape and double-check each figure. With a large garden, inaccuracy of a few inches is not usually critical, but in a small garden an already cramped patio that gets reduced by another foot may become unusable.

Jot every detail down on paper. Take notes and make little sketches. It is surprising how much you forget when you are back inside drawing the plan to scale. If it is raining or blowing a gale, stay indoors and wait until it stops. Wet paper blowing about in the wind is not the best condition for accuracy. Use an indelible pen in case it starts to rain during the work. A clear plastic cover for the sheet of paper is a useful extra.

Start with the boundaries. Get them marked down. If the sides are at right angles it is easy, but if some of the sides meet at a smaller or greater angle, make sure that the finished lines representing all the sides actually connect at the corners. Now take a point that is part of the boundary. It could be the corner where two walls meet, or any other focal point. Take all the measurements from this datum point. This will allow you to pinpoint accurately any feature, such as manhole, tree, or path.

Where there is sun and shade, hatch in the shaded areas and avoid them when positioning the patio, greenhouse, and fruit garden. Take note of areas in shade or where there is a cold draught funnelled between two buildings. Are there strips along the base of walls where the roof eaves overhang and the soil is

always dry? Make a note. What areas are most in public view? How important is it to include screening for privacy and/or shelter? Mark in the compass positions. In the northern hemisphere, south- and west-facing will have good aspects, north- and east-facing not so good.

Differences in level should be noted; where the ground slopes, mark the fall between A and B. Use a spirit level and straight edge to take levels and note heights and hollows.

A cool head is needed to sort out the new design and take the garden forward. Appraise what is already growing. Where there are good, well-grown plants on site it may be worth trying to accommodate them into your design. Remember that where there is limited access, everything that can be allowed to remain without compromising the design will save time, money, and effort. Some of the plants may be kept for a few seasons with the advantage that they will add an air of maturity when all the new planting is small. It can be great moving into a property with a brand-new garden that is a blank, albeit small, canvas. With it you can immediately mark out the features you want to have and see how they fit.

Mark in any existing features. Include any plants that are being retained, walls, hard surfaces, obstacles, manholes, downpipe guttering, and so on. Decide whether any features are to be discarded. Old, unwanted plants can be dug out by the root and shredded; mark them on the plan with an x or, if you are absolutely

## CHECK-LIST OF PREFERENCES

- Secret garden

- Vegetable patch

- Play area (safe and secure)

- Patio in sheltered sunny spot

- Flowers for cutting

- Garden seat

sure they and their roots are for the chop, leave them out of the plan altogether. A manhole that is unlikely to be regularly inspected may be disguised with a layer of gravel or ground-covering plants; be sure to mark its position clearly on the drawing. It would be annoying if it suddenly became part of the patio or ended up buried under decking.

With the boundaries and permanent features drawn, now design your garden.

Decide on a suitable scale that will fit the sheet of paper, and then draw the plan. For small areas, a scale of 1:50 or 1:100 is usually ideal. 1:50 means that each inch marked on the plan represents 50in of the garden. 1:100 is double that, i.e. each inch represents 100in.

Using a pencil to make the drawing will allow changes to be easily implemented. Start with the "must-haves" and place them in their ideal position. At this stage it is not important to do too detailed a plan. A hatched area may represent a small bed of scented plants; the actual plants need not be listed. It is more important that the bed reserved is large enough for what you have in mind.

It's a good idea to double-check, so now mark out your plan on the ground. Use dry sand or a spray-canister marker

ABOVE: *Note measurements of all main features to make sure they will fit into the allotted space.*

to set out the features to scale. Don't be
tempted to use a hose. In small areas it
isn't sufficiently flexible to set out the
detailed plan accurately, and in winter it
is difficult to make good curves. Again,
get a friend to hold the other end of the
measuring tape. Drive in wooden pegs to
mark the corners of large features, such
as a patio. The path should be accurately
marked, as all the other features will
be positioned around it. Scratch a line
using a pointed stick or spade to mark
curves for beds and borders. When you
are sure the curve looks right, fix its
position with the sand or marker. Where
the property is two-story and the garden
may be viewed from above, check the
curves from upper windows. The curve
that seems ideal at ground level will
appear completely different from above.
Again, help will be needed to make the
alterations at ground level.

Where a circle has to be made, drive
a wooden peg into the ground at the
point where you want its center to be.
Tie a string on a loose loop to the peg
about a foot above ground level. Tie the
other end to a pointed peg. The distance
between the two pegs should be the
radius (half the diameter) of the circle.
Keep the string tight and mark a line
on the ground as you move around the
center peg. Alternatively, tie the string at
the correct length to the spray canister
and mark the line using that.

Where you need a right angle to set
out a patio or decking, make yourself
a right-angled former: cut three pieces
of timber lath exactly 3ft, 4ft and 5ft in
length and fix them to form a triangle.
(In a right-angled triangle, the sum of
the squares of the two short sides equals
the square of the long side, i.e. (3 x 3) +
(4 x 4) = (5 x 5).)

## REASSESSING

Stand in the garden and look at the result. Walk the walk. Get a feel for what it will be. Leave it for a few days while keeping a watch on the weather. Is the sitting and entertaining area in a sunny position, or is it shaded for a large part of the day? Look out from inside the dwelling. Will screening plants give you privacy and shelter, or will they block the view? At the moment it is still easy to make changes. Is the patio going to be large enough? Is the bed when planted going to make the garden seem smaller by drawing your attention to the near end of the site? Does the path need to be wider, or would stepping-stones be more practical? Make alterations on the ground as necessary and transfer the corrections back to the plan.

Where it becomes obvious that you are running out of usable space, sit down, or stand up, and reassess your wish list. Where can you save space? Do you really want a small lawn and a patio? Would a portable barbecue do instead of a built-in permanent feature? Biting the bullet and making hard decisions now is better than later having to undo work already carried out.

LEFT: *Mark out your plan using dry sand in a plastic bottle or a spray-canister marker.*

## DETAILS AND EXTRAS

Many details need to be taken into account when you are designing. If you overlook certain components at the beginning, they may be difficult to work into the scheme when the plan is being implemented. Where a contractor is carrying out the work, extras—such as edgings to paths and handrails—tend to be expensive.

Edgings to paths, especially those with a gravel surface, may be timber, brick, or stone; in any case they should be included in the plan. Handrails where there are steep steps leading down from pavement level are essential for safety and will be requested by your local building-control department. For wheelchair access, the need for a ramp from the garden to one entrance to the dwelling will also be stipulated. Where the patio or decking is above the rest of the garden, a sturdy timber or wrought-iron railing is advisable.

If required, outside power points need to be installed and armored cables laid underground before other work is undertaken. An outside water supply is important; think about where it should best be positioned so you won't have to drag the hose through plants. Where an automatic watering system is being installed, select a central point for the delivery lines.

# Chapter 6—
# Case studies

While it would be impossible to cover every conceivable garden situation, there are general rules and hints and tips that are common to certain garden types. The rooftop and balcony garden will be more prone to adverse weather conditions than a basement or back yard. Where there is no soil to garden in, containers and raised beds offer a suitable solution. Parking off-road is desirable these days, yet it would be a shame to sacrifice the front garden. With good design, both are compatible. Whatever your particular situation, with a little common sense you will be able to find enough space to garden in.

# OFF-STREET CAR PARK

**Site conditions:** Whole of front garden has been turned into a car park. Gravel surface over hardcore. Not a single plant.

**Size:** 26ft x 23ft

**Client's brief:** Bachelor with no time for gardening. He would like a few plants that are low-maintenance, and a screen along the road side. Something nice at the front door.

**Problems:** Soil is a mixture of clay and builder's debris. Space needed to open car doors.

## Solution

Matching spiral-shaped golden conifers will provide year-round interest and color while only requiring the odd snip with secateurs to retain their shape. Forming raised beds in the two corners allows you to plant in imported topsoil. The evergreen berberis hedge offers some privacy from passers-by. The *Thuja plicata* hedges will offer screening to the front door and make an interesting entrance from the car park. Gravel laid on landscape fabric will keep weeding to a minimum.

TOP: *An edging of lavender will not only look good, the aromatic leaves and flowers will be appreciated in a roadside setting.*
BOTTOM: *Where the parking area is surfaced in gravel, stepping-stones will show you where to walk.*

# FRONT GARDEN OFF-STREET CAR PARK

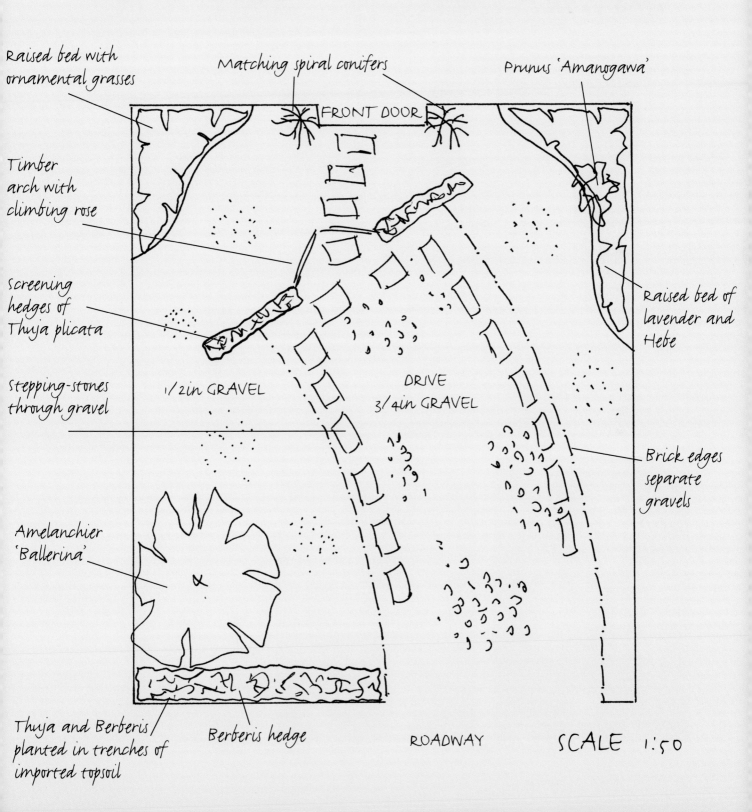

Raised bed with ornamental grasses

Matching spiral conifers

Prunus 'Amanogawa'

FRONT DOOR

Timber arch with climbing rose

screening hedges of Thuja plicata

stepping-stones through gravel

1/2in GRAVEL

DRIVE 3/4in GRAVEL

Raised bed of lavender and Hebe

Brick edges separate gravels

Amelanchier 'Ballerina'

Thuja and Berberis planted in trenches of imported topsoil

Berberis hedge

ROADWAY

SCALE 1:50

# NARROW FRONT GARDEN

**Site conditions:** Down side of house to porch entrance. Concrete paving-slab surface. No plants. Unsightly water and sewage pipes down high wall. Sun all day.

**Size:** 30ft x 7.5ft

**Client's brief:** Family including two teenage boys. No gardening knowledge. Make the approach to the front door more inviting. Hide the pipework. Conceal two bicycles.

**Problems:** No soil. Very windy.

### Solution

Attaching wire mesh to the unsightly downpipes allows climbing plants to scramble up and make them disappear. Dividing the garden with the planted parallel timber trellis blocks a view of the porch and leaves a screened sitting area and bicycle park. All the specimen shrubs and climbers are planted in containers. The small raised bed offers salads and herbs for the kitchen. The mixture of gravel, river stones, and sandstone paving breaks up the garden, making it look wider.

LEFT: *Large areas of Indian sandstone can be broken up with lines of rustic red brick.*
FAR LEFT: *Lonicera henryi is evergreen, providing year-round privacy.*

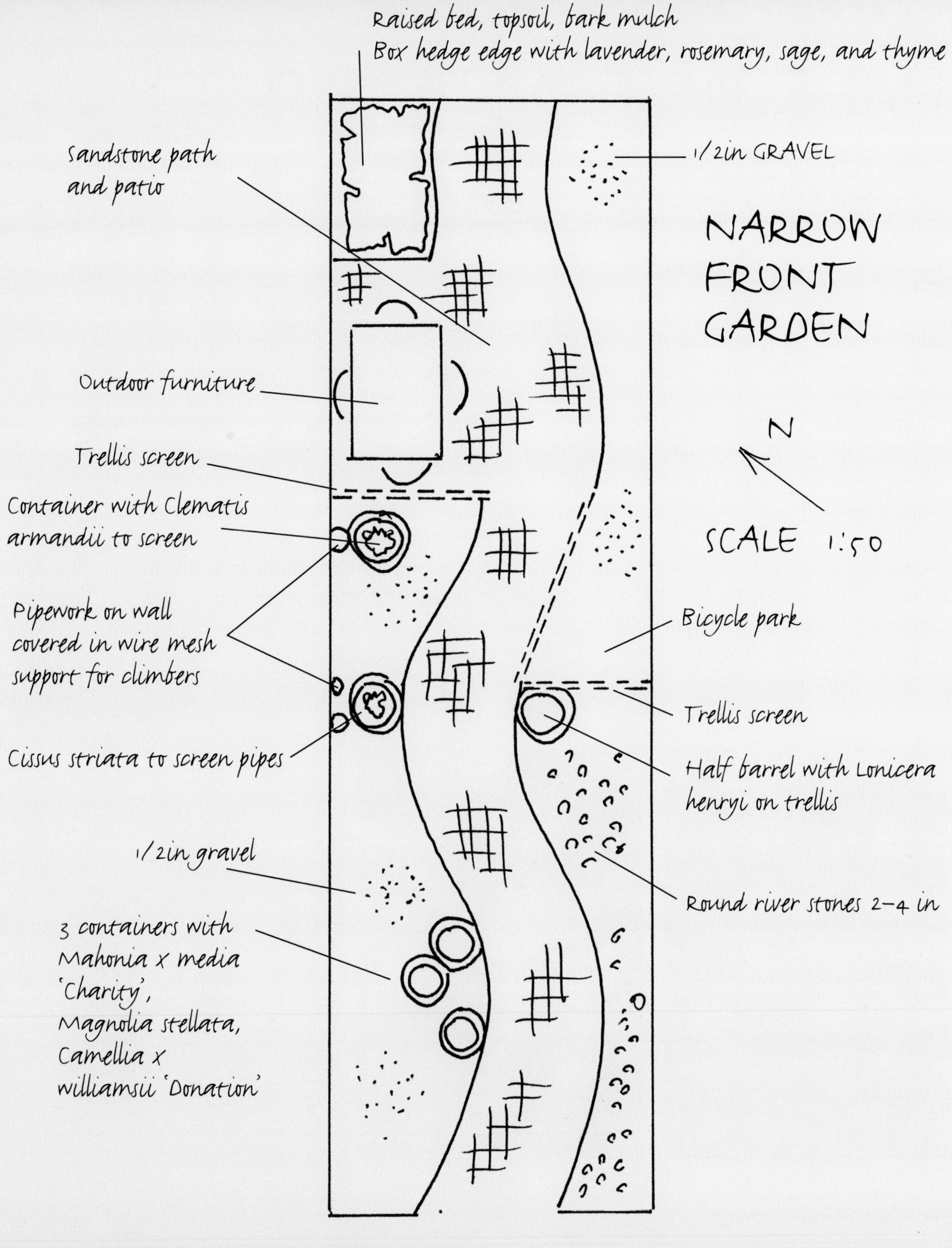

Raised bed, topsoil, bark mulch
Box hedge edge with lavender, rosemary, sage, and thyme

Sandstone path
and patio

1/2in GRAVEL

NARROW
FRONT
GARDEN

Outdoor furniture

N

Trellis screen

SCALE 1:50

Container with Clematis
armandii to screen

Pipework on wall
covered in wire mesh
support for climbers

Bicycle park

Trellis screen

Half barrel with Lonicera
henryi on trellis

Cissus striata to screen pipes

1/2in gravel

Round river stones 2-4 in

3 containers with
Mahonia x media
'Charity',
Magnolia stellata,
Camellia x
williamsii 'Donation'

# BALCONY

**Site conditions:** Very basic. Previous owner never used it. A few plastic pots with ivy. Concrete floor. Sunny but also windy. Second floor.

**Size:** 9ft x 5.5ft

**Client's brief:** A retired couple, active and keen gardeners. Would like year-round plant color and interest. Mostly permanent planting. Table and two chairs for alfresco eating. Fragrance.

**Problems:** Materials have to be carried to second floor and through the apartment. Need to provide shelter from wind without causing shade. Also need pots large enough to hold soil mix to sustain long-term planting.

### Solution

The timber trellis and arch will support fragrant summer-flowering climbers, such as honeysuckle and roses. *Loniceras fragrantissima* flowers in winter with scented flowers. *Sarcococca confusa* will dish out winter perfume. The evergreen *Clematis armandii,* with white perfumed flowers in early spring, can be trained through the railing, cutting the wind. Tiling the floor will dispense with the boring concrete.

LEFT: *Where there is space to grow clematis, it is great for winding its way in and out of balcony railings.*
FAR LEFT: *Sarcococca confusa gives you evergreen foliage, incredible winter perfume from the small white flowers and attractive berries in spring.*

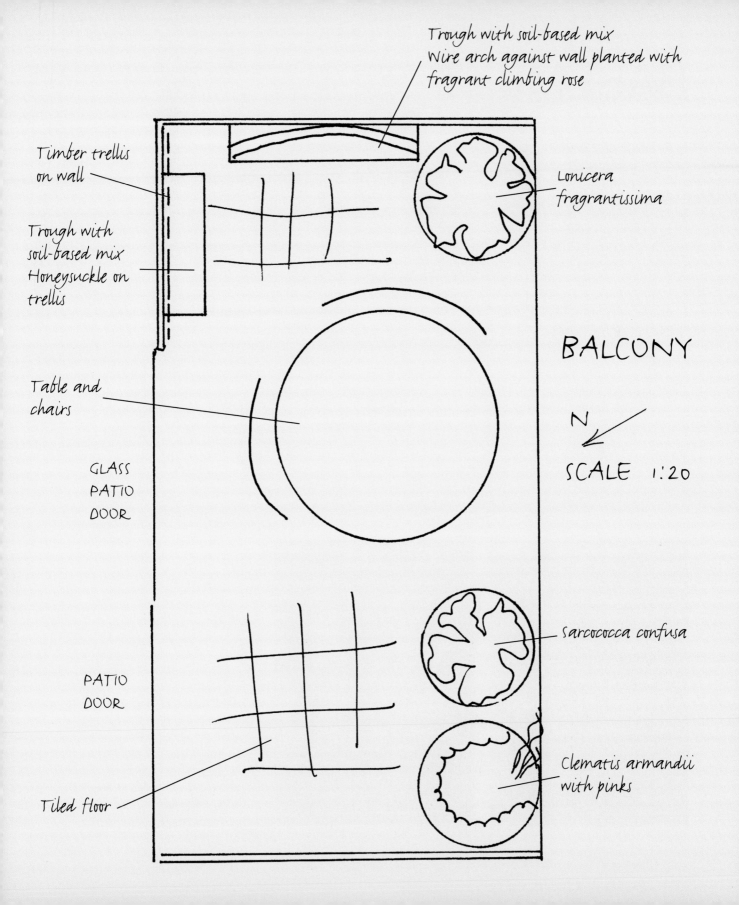

Trough with soil-based mix
Wire arch against wall planted with
fragrant climbing rose

Timber trellis
on wall

Trough with
soil-based mix
Honeysuckle on
trellis

Lonicera
fragrantissima

Table and
chairs

GLASS
PATIO
DOOR

BALCONY

N

SCALE 1:20

PATIO
DOOR

Sarcococca confusa

Tiled floor

Clematis armandii
with pinks

# BASEMENT

**Site conditions:** Old house in city, badly overgrown with old garden plants. Front of house with quarter of the floor area and one wall getting morning sun.

**Size:** 12ft x 8ft

**Client's brief:** Family with two children under 6. Would love some privacy and an area for children's play equipment. Low-maintenance garden. No poisonous plants.

**Problems:** Existing wall plants growing in heavy clay soil. Very shaded and very public.

### Solution
The sunny part has been given over to trained apple trees and scented jasmine on the walls with tile and thyme patio surface. The bamboo won't mind the heavy soil and will provide much needed screening for part of the patio. The white sail awning stretched from wall to wall and secured to stainless steel hooks will provide privacy to the play area while acting as an umbrella in wet weather. There is a small raised bed of shade-loving plants.

LEFT: *Bamboo planted as a screening hedge.*
FAR LEFT: *Chaenomeles (ornamental quince) can be trained on a wall and is tolerant to shade.*

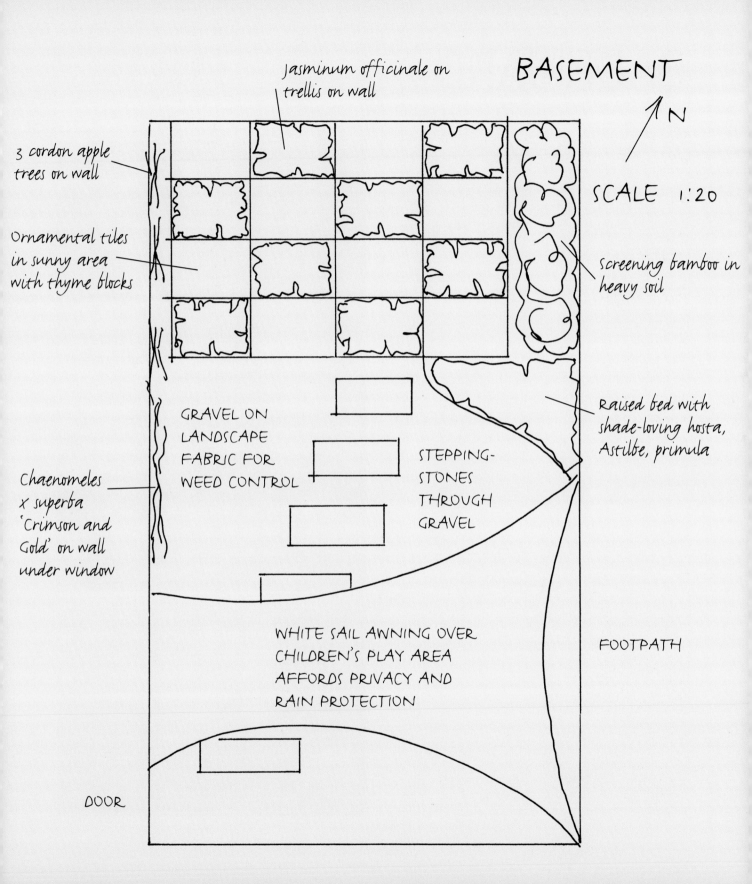

Jasminum officinale on trellis on wall

BASEMENT

N

SCALE 1:20

3 cordon apple trees on wall

Ornamental tiles in sunny area with thyme blocks

screening bamboo in heavy soil

Chaenomeles x superba 'Crimson and Gold' on wall under window

GRAVEL ON LANDSCAPE FABRIC FOR WEED CONTROL

STEPPING-STONES THROUGH GRAVEL

Raised bed with shade-loving hosta, Astilbe, primula

FOOTPATH

WHITE SAIL AWNING OVER CHILDREN'S PLAY AREA AFFORDS PRIVACY AND RAIN PROTECTION

DOOR

# BACK YARD

**Site conditions:** Previously used to store tools, coal, and a rabbit hutch. Base is concrete slabs over mass concrete. Walls 8ft high with kitchen window and door in one wall, with the exit from the back garden opposite.

**Size:** 11ft x 10ft.

**Client's brief:** Couple in 40s. No children. They want to entertain and would like to grow some salads and have interesting shrubs.

**Problems:** High perimeter walls cause lots of shade. Solid floor. Wall support needed for climbers.

## Solution

All the plants are in containers. Edible crops are grown in mangers supported on the sunny wall. When entertaining, the home-grown pears, peaches, and grapes will be a talking point. Raised decking will hide the concrete floor while the sound and sight of running water will be soothing. The remainder of the floor will look warm with sandstone tiles. Evergreen climbing hydrangea and the pineapple scented flowers of *Cytisus* (pineapple broom) will be interesting.

Top: *Grow your own: it doesn't just have to be tomatoes or radishes.*
Bottom: *Cytisus battandieri is better known as pineapple broom, with silvery green foliage and bright yellow flowers that smell of pineapple.*

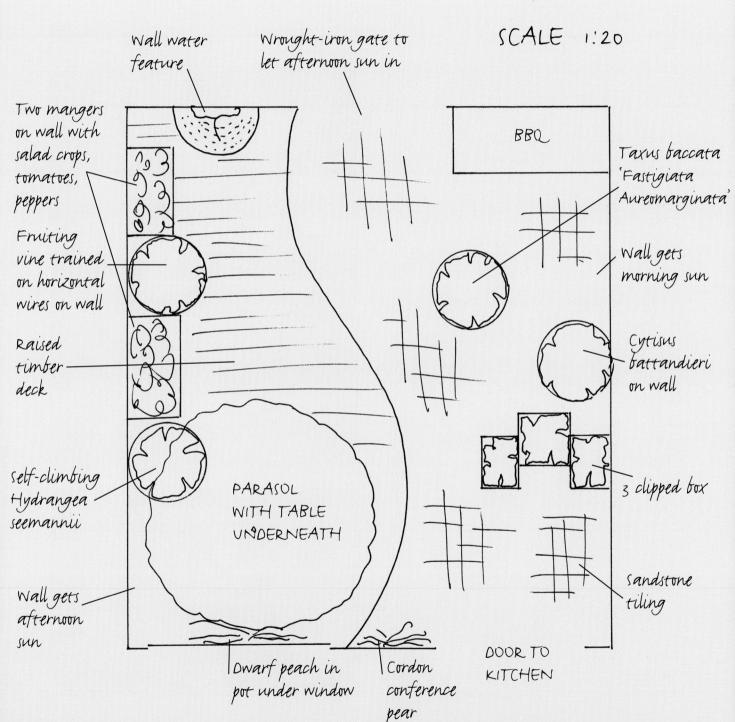

BACK YARD

N

SCALE 1:20

Wall water feature

Wrought-iron gate to let afternoon sun in

BBQ

Two mangers on wall with salad crops, tomatoes, peppers

Taxus baccata 'Fastigiata Aureomarginata'

Fruiting vine trained on horizontal wires on wall

Wall gets morning sun

Raised timber deck

Cytisus battandieri on wall

self-climbing Hydrangea seemannii

PARASOL WITH TABLE UNDERNEATH

3 clipped box

Wall gets afternoon sun

sandstone tiling

Dwarf peach in pot under window

Cordon conference pear

DOOR TO KITCHEN

# ROOF GARDEN

**Site conditions:** New site. Exposed. Asphalt floor. Has building approval for a garden. Two high walls, one in shade.

**Size:** 13ft x 16ft.

**Client's brief:** Single lady. Privacy for sunbathing essential. Would like furniture for entertaining. Low-maintenance garden.

**Problems:** Windy. There's no screening for privacy on the sides without walls.

## Solution

A long raised bed with a soil-based mix will accommodate tough screening plants such as bamboo, *Phormium* (New Zealand flax), and *Elaeagnus*. Containers planted with Aucuba (spotted laurel), Ulex (double-flowering gorse), and *Kalmia* (mountain laurel) will offer color and shelter. An automatic watering system will reduce maintenance. Reinforced glass will provide shelter for sunbathing.

TOP: *Kalmia latifolia, or mountain laurel, is as tough as old boots. In bud, the flowers resemble cake decorations.*
BOTTOM: *Gravel is attractive and practical—just make sure the roof can withstand the load.*

# ROOF GARDEN

SCALE 1:50 ↘ N

Aucuba japonica 'Crotonifolia'

Gravel

Ulex europaeus

Kalmia latifolia

DOOR

Railings with reinforced glass panels 4ft high

Tiled floor for table, sunshade, chairs, lounger

Planted with bamboo, Phormium, Elaeagnus, evergreen oak

2ft raised bed with timber sides and soil-based mix
Automatic watering

# Part 2: making it happen

The timescale can be all-important. If the structural work is contracted out, the landscaper will be able to quote you a finish date subject to adverse weather conditions. A do-it-yourself operation will take longer. Allow more time than you think necessary. As well as doing the work, you have to source and collect materials and plants. If you are not retired, your day job may rule out any work during the week—especially in winter when it gets dark early in the evening.

It would be nice if the bulk of the work could be completed before the Easter period, allowing the latter part of spring and summer for relaxing and entertaining while admiring the finished job and watching your garden grow.

In the case of small gardens, such as balconies and rooftop gardens where access is restricted, materials will have to be carried through the house. To avoid too much upheaval and potential mess, award the contract or undertake the work yourself when the weather is dry.

# Chapter 7—
# Structural components

When all the pieces of the plan come together, you can then consider doing the actual work and making your design a reality. Don't worry if you have not got the plan exactly as you want your garden to finish up. It is not, and most likely never will be, set in stone. Most gardens evolve; as long as the basics are right, the detail may change at any time. As you conjure up better plant selections and improved design ideas they can be accommodated on site.

# Construction

With a small garden where everything is on a modest scale, it is perfectly feasible for you to do some, most, or even all of the work yourself. Drafting in a few strong friends to help with the donkey work may cost you no more than a case of beer!

However, don't be tempted to take short cuts. If you are over-running your allocated time, so be it. Rushing the job may lead to tears, postponed work, and poor workmanship, resulting in a loss of enthusiasm, drive, and interest. Remember that the garden is small. Mistakes will be noticed, especially where levels are incorrect and steps and slopes appear that weren't on the plan. Rectifying problems later when most of the work is complete may involve a lot of extra expense.

If you balk at the hard-surfacing of paths and patios, along with erecting fences and building walls, pergolas, or ponds, contract out that part of the work while retaining the physical planting for yourself. As with the design, you can pay a landscape contractor to do the work to your plan. Using a professional has the advantages of a probable earlier completion date and work that will be guaranteed.

List the components that will require skilled labor for construction, such as a water feature, pergola, patio, decking, lighting, rock garden, or fencing. Invite quotations for each job from professional and preferably recommended landscape contractors.

Construction is one of those aspects of gardening that you are either capable of or hopeless at. It is not gardening as we know it, and the skills are not gardening skills, but so many elements make up the modern garden that building and joinery know-how is useful. It is worth having a go at some elementary construction work. Pretty quickly you may decide that it is a job for the expert, but at least you won't always wonder whether you could have done all the work yourself.

The golden rule is health and safety first. Don't take short cuts and never use cheap, shoddy materials. If you, rather than a landscape contractor, are carrying out the work, bear in mind expenses that will be incurred over and above the materials bill. You may have to hire specialist equipment, such as a power saw and vibrator plate for laying hard-surface patios. An electric drill with extension cable will be essential for fitting vine eyes and timber trellis to walls. A pneumatic drill will take the hard work out of breaking up old concrete foundations and the base

of paths. A skip will be needed for the removal of debris. There will also be the expense of protective clothing, which may well be a one-off. Always use ear-protectors, goggles, safety helmet, protective gloves, and footwear as necessary.

ABOVE: *For paths and patios, a 6in deep hardcore base is essential, especially where winters are harsh. Consolidate the stone before laying the surface.*
OPPOSITE: *Decking, reconstituted stone slabs, and square setts come together to provide a mixture of smooth and textured surfaces.*

# Hard surfaces

Hard-surface patios and paths may well already be in the only suitable position but need to be renewed. Before ripping out the existing feature, check whether the levels can be raised by a few inches, in which case the original may well suffice as a foundation. You may be able to lay the new surface directly on top, thus saving time and money without having to remove and bring in hardcore.

It may be possible to clean up an old patio or deck surface. Power hosing may remove the old grouting between paving slabs, but it should clean the surface and then it will be a simple job to re-grout the gaps. Providing the timber is sound, power sanding the existing decking may make it as good as new.

Where a hard-surface patio, path, or base for a shed is being removed to be replaced with plants, it is more than likely that there is a sub-base of hardcore that will need to be dug out and disposed of. That may result in your having to import new topsoil to make up the levels before planting. It is a good idea to have all the features clear in your mind. There may well be another site where some hardcore could be used, which will save having to cart it out and bring more back into the garden. A new path or a rock garden area may be in need of a firm base, and a quick trip with the wheelbarrow could save a mountain of work.

## LAYING A PATIO
### Tools required

The essential equipment for laying a patio will be a spirit level, straight edge, line, soft brush, shovel, rake, rubber mallet, pointing trowel, club hammer, and bolster. Where slabs have to be cut, a power saw should be hired. Full protective clothing with boots, gloves, goggles, and ear-protectors finish the list.

### Construction

On your plan there will be a shape representing the patio. Now is the time to check that the marked position is where you want it. The patio is not going to be in demand if it is in a cold, windy, or shaded spot—so is it in a sunny, sheltered position? Is there space to make it the size drawn, or have other aspects of the garden encroached to squeeze it? Is the actual size sufficient for your needs including garden furniture? Is the site level or, if not, can it be made flat without a lot of raising or lowering of ground?

Use a spray marker or a line of sand to mark the patio boundaries. Where a plant bed has been designed into the patio, mark it out on the ground. This will save a lot of digging out and replacing of soil later. Make sure it isn't out of proportion to the patio and won't make positioning the furniture difficult. Where the patio is up against a house wall, it must be below the damp-proof course (DPC), if present.

Check that the site is level. I don't mean just look at it and imagine it is OK. Use a spirit level and a long timber straight edge or taut string. Drive a wooden peg into the ground at one side, leaving 2–3in exposed. Now rest one end of a perfectly straight length of

timber on the peg and level it, using the spirit level. That will give you an idea of how level the ground is. Drive in pegs along the other sides of the marked-out patio and level them to the original peg. Tie a line tightly across the site of the patio in several directions from the tops of the pegs. This will show the differences in height, and how much the area needs to be raised or lowered.

The finished level should have a small fall across the finished surface, away from any building, to allow rainwater to run off. A slope of 2in in 12–15ft will be adequate without affecting the stability of furniture.

You will need to dig down to firm subsoil before laying the hardcore base. A stone base laid on soft soil will eventually sink, causing all sorts of problems. If the stripped topsoil is good, stockpile it for later use for raised beds and making up levels throughout the garden. The patio is only for pedestrian traffic rather than a landing pad for helicopters, so 6–8in of consolidated 2in crusher-run stone will be sufficient. Hire a walk-behind vibrator to consolidate the hardcore to make the base solid.

Use dry sand to get an even finished level and, once the base has been vibrated, the patio surface may be laid on top. Where bricks are being used without grouting, lay them directly on the sand. When they are all placed, brush fine, dry sand over the surface and into the cracks. Another light run over the patio with the vibrator settles the sand into the gaps.

Either lay slabs and tiles on a bed of mortar, or place each tile on 5 dollops of mortar and tap into place with the rubber mallet. Keep the gaps between the slabs the same width. Frequent checks with the level and keeping the

tiles up to the height-line will prevent dips or humps from appearing.

Providing the surface is dry the following day, with no rain expected for a few hours, grout between the tiles using a dry mix of cement and sand, four parts sand to one part cement by bulk. Brush the mixture into the spaces between the slabs using a soft brush. Brush off the excess, making sure you remove any from lines or raised edges on tiles with a ridged surface. Within two days the cement-sand mixture will have absorbed moisture and set hard.

Where the patio design shows curved edges, mark the line you will cut to. Make sure there are no small corners of tiles left on the outside edge. Small pieces are difficult to secure and usually work loose unless held in place with edging.

Kerb edging is best installed before the patio; it can be used to set the levels all round. Secure it in place with concrete, keeping the concrete low enough to leave space for the tile or slab to sit on top.

**1** Thoroughly mix the mortar with sufficient water to form a dryish base.

**2** Use a rubber mallet to level the slab.

**3** A timber straight edge and spirit level is constantly in use to check levels.

**4** Brush or trowel a dry mix of sand and cement into the spaces between the tiles.

## MAKING A TIMBER DECK

### Tools required

Spirit level, hammer, screws, power screwdriver, power drill, carriage bolts, hand saw, spade. Where the deck is large and there is a considerable amount of cutting to be done, a power saw will speed up the work. When using power tools in the garden, make sure they are connected to the electric supply through a ground fault interrupter. Protective clothing, including goggles, gloves, and ear-protectors, is essential. All timbers (apart from western red ceder) need to be preserved, preferably by pressure treatment that forces the chemical into the wood.

### Construction

As with a patio, it is important that decking is level. There is no need to have a slight fall, as water can run off between the planks. Where there is a pre-determined height, such as when the decking is to finish flush with an outdoor step or one step lower, that becomes the datum point from which all other levels are taken. The depth of the surface timber plus the depth of the joists is the total clearance needed.

There is no need to excavate and form a hardcore base below the decking, but the joists should be clear of the ground to prevent them from retaining moisture. What's underneath the deck won't be seen, but spreading a layer of landscape fabric and pegging it down will prevent weeds from growing up through the deck.

Upright 4in x 4in timber posts need to be concreted 18in into the ground approximately 6ft apart along all four sides of the decking. The finished height of the posts should be 2in higher than the datum point. Use a spirit level to make sure the posts are vertical, and use a cord line to position them in straight lines. Run two lines at right angles to make sure the front and sides are square. (See page 104.)

If the deck area is larger than 6ft x 6ft, concrete more posts in between the opposite sides, in line with the outer posts and at a spacing of 2m or less. When the posts are in place, smooth the top of the concrete with a pointing

**HOW TO MAKE A TIMBER DECK**

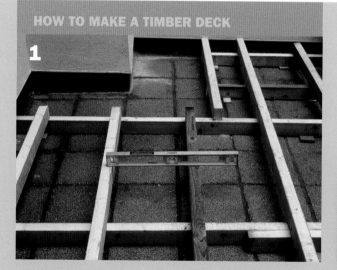

**1** Make sure the frame or joists are level, otherwise the decking will be warped, or bounce when walked on.

**2** Cut decking to lengths that allow ends to rest on a joist.

trowel so that it slopes away from each post without leaving a depression where water could collect and rot the timber.

After the concrete has set, use carriage bolts to secure the joists to the uprights, the thickness of the decking below the datum point. Run the joists in the opposite direction to the way you want the deck timbers to be laid. Check frequently that they are level and all at the same height. A line fixed at either end of an outside joist and carried across to the opposite joist means that the in-between timbers will be level if they just touch the taut cord. Cut the ends of the joists flush with the outside edge of the posts.

Now reduce the height of the supporting posts so they are level with the top of the joists. Lay the deck timbers across the joists. If they are unsteady or rock, either the planks are warped and should be returned to the supplier, or at least one of the joists is out of line with the others. When you are satisfied that the deck planks are resting on all the joists, screw them in place, fixing 2 screws into each joist. Using a cord across the planks, along the line of the center of the joist, allows you to position the screws in a straight line (the finished job looks better). Space the planks evenly using ½in-wide blocks of wood as spacers.

The sides and leading edge of the decking can be covered with decking planks screwed to the ends of the joists and the upright posts. Where there is more than one step leading down from the decking, fit a safety handrail.

Where the decking is to be laid on a balcony or rooftop floor, construct a timber frame on the floor and make it level using batons of wood. Firmly screw the joists to the framework and fix the decking on top, as before. Never be tempted to nail or screw through into the roof or you may have an unwanted water feature!

Where plant containers are part of the decking furniture, raise them on "feet" to prevent them from staining the timber.

**3** Hand-nail, screw, or power-staple the timbers to the joists.

**4** The finished decking should be without cracks or gaps.

## HOW TO LAY A PATH

**1** Roughly mark the shape of the path using a hose. Dig out the loose soil.

**2** Lay hardcore base and sand. Compact the surface and level.

**3** Lay bricks without gaps.

**4** Level with rubber mallet or club hammer on a wooden baton.

**5** Brush dry sand on to the surface to fill cracks.

**6** Fit for purpose.

## PATHS AND STEPPING-STONES

Having decided where the path is to be, mark out the line on the ground. Depending on the finished surface, some form of sub-base will be required. The heaviest things it will have to support will be people and a wheelbarrow. Unless the ground is very soft, excavating 6in of topsoil and laying 4in of ½in gravel will prevent the path from sinking. Use a vibrator to consolidate the hardcore base and level it off with a 1in layer of sand. Lay the slabs as for the patio (see page 125). Gravel paths should be surfaced with 3/8–½in gravel, either broken stone or river-washed pebbles.

In a small garden, the path width should be kept to a minimum. While it would be nice to have the luxury of two people being able to walk side by side, the waste of space is hard to justify.

Gravel paths will need an edging to retain the stones. A line or hedge of dwarf plants, such as box or lavender, on either side will frame the path.

Stepping-stones may be used to cross a small lawn or a shrub bed. Annual bedding plants or carpeting plants may be grown between the slabs. Make sure that the stepping-stones are firmly bedded on a mortar base and are spaced for ease of walking. Spaces of 12in between slabs are generally satisfactory for most grown-ups.

RIGHT: *Timber surrounds work best if they are substantial. If they are sufficiently wide you can sit on the edge.*

## RAISED BEDS

Don't make the beds too wide: 4–5ft is about right, allowing you to reach the plants in the middle from either side. The sides may be made of planks of timber, 10in high and 2in thick. Avoid using old railway sleepers that have been impregnated with tar to help preserve them. New sleeper-like baulks of timber are expensive but look good.

Old scaffolding planks are often available from builders, and these again make walls 8–10in high. Hold them in place by driving in timber pegs and nailing the planks to the pegs. Or you may raise the beds using new timber, but be sure to paint it with a plant-friendly preservative.

As an alternative to timber planks, the sides of the raised bed can be made of bricks or concrete blocks, 10in high, stood on firm ground, end to end, without a foundation or mortar joints. Dwarf walls of local, natural stone are attractive but take up more space than timber sides.

You can erect barriers around a raised bed to prevent pests, such as carrot root fly from laying their eggs. Vaseline smeared along the top edge of a raised bed will act as a barrier to slugs and snails. Laying a sheet of landscape fabric on top of diseased soil before bringing in the new topsoil will reduce the risk of roots picking up diseases, such as club root.

Where you are forced to grow in raised beds because the existing surface is concrete or tarmac, it will be worth spreading a 1in-deep layer of washed gravel in the base of the bed. This will help drainage. Spread on top of the gravel a 3in-deep layer of old, well-rotted farmyard manure to retain moisture,

followed by good-quality, weed-free topsoil. If the soil is heavy, open it up by mixing in some horticultural grit.

Check the quality of any topsoil being delivered. Make sure it is from a reliable source and is free of perennial weed roots. Keep the surface of the topsoil 1in below the rim to prevent soil from being washed over the sides when you are watering. This will also allow room for a mulch to inhibit weeds and help retain moisture in the soil. Proprietary soil mixes may be used, but their consistency encourages them to dry out in summer.

Where long-term shrubs, such as rhododendrons and roses, are being planted, the bed can be mounded in the center to provide an extra few centimetres of depth.

If you line the inside of the frame of the raised bed with polythene before filling with a humus-rich soil, it will be possible to grow plants that thrive in boggy conditions. A few drainage holes punched in the sides of the lining will prevent the bed from becoming a swamp.

# Ponds and water features

## EXISTING WATER FEATURE

Renovating an existing disused pond or water feature is risky. First, make sure it isn't leaking and that the pump works. Get the electricity supply checked by a qualified electrician. Rather than trying to locate and repair a leak, you may do better to drain the pond and fit a new 25-year-guaranteed liner sheet on top of the existing liner. While work is in progress, store the pond water; then replace it when the pond is relined. It will be better than tap water and will be full of creepy-crawlies that will help maintain the water balance and keep it clean.

## POWER SUPPLY

Lay power cables and water piping before undertaking any other work in a new garden. With balconies and rooftop gardens these will have to be above ground and securely clipped to walls.

Where the armored power cable is being brought underground to the water feature, dig the trench 2ft deep. Lay the cable and cover with 2in of sand. Lay a yellow polythene warning strip 8in below the soil surface directly above the cable. Then if anyone is digging in the area they will have warning long before they are at the depth of the cable. Pumps are often supplied with long cables that would easily reach to an existing power outlet, but don't be tempted to run the unprotected cable directly to the power. The cable must be safe from sharp spades and other gardening tools.

## SIZE MATTERS

For an open pond, the hole should be deep enough to allow plants to be grown; 18in deep will be sufficient. A shelf formed on one side or all round the pond 6–8in deep will accommodate marginal plants in containers that like their feet to be in the water. Where a submersible pump is to be installed, one area of the pond needs to be 2ft deep.

### Construction

Remove any stones projecting from the base or sides of the excavated hole, and vibrate the base to prevent subsidence or compaction caused by the weight of water. Cover the sides and base with sand or pond underlay to prevent sharp objects from puncturing the liner. Where a flexible liner is being used it should have a guarantee of 20–25 years.

Work out the size of the liner: measure the length and width of the base of the hole, and add on to each measurement twice the depth and an extra 8in on all sides for the overhang at the top. Before placing the liner in the hole, make a last check to remove any small stones that may have fallen in on top of the sand or underlay. Start to fill the pond with water, pulling the liner tight to remove wrinkles. Where the sides curve or there are corners, form neat pleats in the sides of the liner, folding them to one side.

At this stage only half-fill the pond, as you may want to work standing in it. The water will become contaminated with dust, chippings, and cement during the work and will need to be changed once construction is finished. If you are

TOP: *Colorful pebbles disguise the pump and reservoir, and glisten when wet.*

ABOVE: *For a really small water feature, pump the water from the gravel-covered reservoir to an earthenware dish with a lip.*

OPPOSITE: *The water feature may be no larger than a dinner plate but it will be teeming with wildlife. Birds and frogs will help control slugs and snails.*

wearing boots, make sure there are no small, sharp stones embedded in the soles that could puncture the liner.

Before laying the surrounding finish of tiles or slabs, position the pump with the power cable and the outlet hose. These can be tiled over, but in both cases leave enough slack in the pond to allow the pump to be lifted out of the water for cleaning and maintenance.

Allow the tiles to overhang the edge of the pond by 2–3in, hiding the rim of the black liner that is above the water level. The surrounding tiles might become part of a path, thus saving space.

Pumped water will introduce oxygen to the pond and help prevent it from turning green. Small ponds need pumps that move small amounts of water; it is a mistake to fit a large-capacity pump where there isn't a large volume of water. Where there isn't moving water, you will have to rely on plants adding oxygen to the water. It may take several weeks or months for a balance to be achieved, where insects and plants manage to keep the water clean. The worst thing you can do is change green water: it will eventually clear, whereas changing it will set back the process. Wherever possible, use rainwater to fill the pond. Oxygenating plants help to produce oxygen, but they will quickly grow to fill the pond. By the end of the first season you may have to pull out and compost half of the vegetation.

Water-lilies prefer still water, with no water splashing on the foliage. Read the plant label; each variety will have a recommended planting depth. If those that like to be at a depth of 18in are positioned in 3ft of water they will suffer and refuse to flower.

Filtration systems and ultraviolet lights can be used in conjunction with pumps to deter green water and algae, but even with them you may, during a hot summer, experience discoloration.

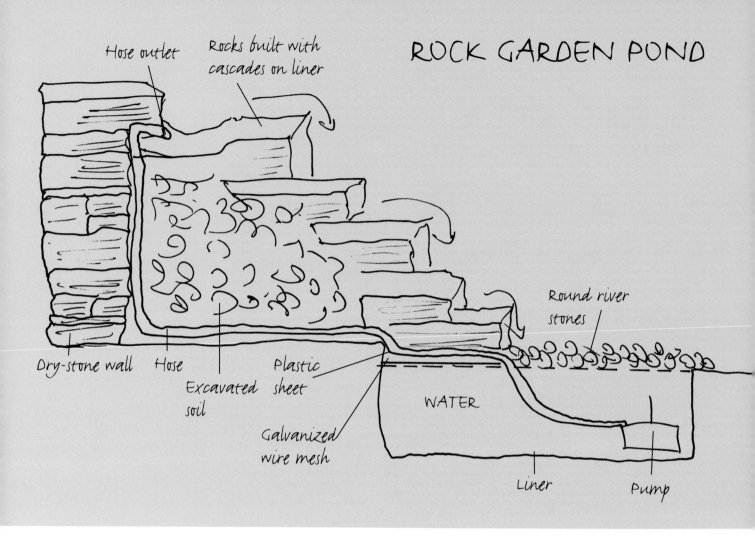

**ROCK GARDEN POND**

Hose outlet

Rocks built with cascades on liner

Dry-stone wall    Hose

Excavated soil

Plastic sheet

Galvanized wire mesh

Round river stones

WATER

Liner    Pump

## WILDLIFE

Where the small garden benefits from wildlife, encourage birds by making a shallow area where the water is less than 2in deep. Form a timber or stone ramp at one side of the pond to provide an escape route for animals that fall in.

Pondweed is dark green and stringy, while duckweed has tiny, bright green leaves and covers the water surface. Both are big trouble, and every effort must be made to eliminate them. Skimming the surface with a fine net will get rid of a lot of the duckweed—but it will return. You can pull out the pondweed using a stick or brush. Both may be put on the compost heap, but first leave them in a pile at the side of the pond for a few hours, to allow insects to crawl back into the water.

## ROCK GARDEN POND

In the small garden there is unlikely to be available space for a rock garden with a torrent of pumped water cascading and crashing back down through rocks to a lower pond.

You may, if so inclined, make a rock pond in miniature, with the whole feature taking up less than 15sq ft.

You will not only enjoy the sight and sound of running water, but also have the opportunity to plant alpines and dwarf bulbs while adding height to the smallest of gardens. And this water feature is safe for children.

Build a dry-stone wall 2ft in height. At a distance of about 2ft in front of it, dig a hole 3ft in diameter and 1ft deep. Line the hole as before (page 130). Position a small submersible pump that will lift 200–250 gallons of water to 3ft in height. Connect a ½in-diameter hose and bring it and the power cable out of the hole. Cover the surface with

galvanized wire mesh, mesh size 2in x ¾in, resting on reinforcing iron rods. Lay plastic sheeting on top of part of the mesh, to cover the rear 12in. Position the hose on top of the plastic, across to and up the inside of the wall. Using rocks to match the wall, build a rock garden on top of the plastic sheeting and back to the wall. Use the excavated topsoil to form pockets of soil for planting between the rocks.

To make the cascades, lay a 12in-wide strip of pool liner from the top of the rock garden between rocks and down to the hole. Make the base of the cascade 6in wide, bending the liner up to form sides. Cover the base and sides with small, flat pieces of rock cemented into place. At the base, position a flat rock horizontally out from the lowest rock and resting on it to overhang the lined hole. This will create a small waterfall.

Wedge the hose outlet between rocks at the top of the rock garden. Cover the remaining 2ft of galvanized mesh with 3–4in-diameter, round, river-washed stone of your choosing. Fill the pond with water. Connect the pump to a power point and switch it on. The water will trickle down over the rocks, disappearing through the stones into the concealed reservoir.

Now finish the job by planting small, slow-growing choice alpines.

With most small water features there is no need to install a complicated overflow outlet leading to a drain. When heavy rain causes the pond to fill, connect one end of an extension hose to the pump outlet and the other end to a drain, and switch the pump on until the level is back to normal.

## MOVING WATER

In a small garden with an even smaller pool, great care has to be taken with the selection of a fountain head. The height of the jet of water must be less than half the width of the catchment area. Wind will blow the water sideways, and if it falls outside the pond the level will fall, emptying the pool and damaging the submersible pump. Use a low-volume pump and try various fountain heads. To prevent the fountain outlets from getting blocked, keep the water clean and regularly clean the filter.

Small, easily installed water features are available as kits in stores and garden centers. Some are contained in a waterproofed wooden barrel, complete with reproduction old-fashioned hand-operated water pump. Others have the water trickling over tiers of metal "leaves", or out of a wall-mounted lion's mouth.

Lights in the garden are magical, and nowhere are they better positioned than to light up and show off moving water. Again, they should be installed by a qualified electrician.

ABOVE: *Many small water features are available as DIY kits but make sure the electrical connection is made by a qualified electrician.*

# Rock garden

A good, well-designed, and well-built rock garden doesn't have to be large. It should resemble in miniature a mountain range, such as the Alps—and it is amazing how many small alpine plants can be accommodated in a 15sq ft rock area.

Select an area that is away from shade. A steep slope may be used, or the rock garden can be made from excavated subsoil from a patio or path with a few inches of gritty, free-draining soil on top.

Whenever possible, use rock that is local to the area. Where there are strata lines, as with sandstone, make sure that all the pieces of rock have them running in the same direction. The finished rock garden should look natural, almost as if the rocks had grown out of the ground.

The golden rule is to use topsoil that is free of perennial weed roots or weed seeds. There is a law stating that the worst weeds will be centered under the largest rock and impossible to get at.

Lay the rocks close together, and position them firmly without any rocking or movement. Fill the small pockets between them with free-draining soil that has not been fertilized. Build up the rocks with a tilt towards the rear to allow rainwater to run back on to the root zone of the lower plants.

Vertical cracks and gaps between rocks may be filled with soil and planted with alpines, such as *Lewisia cotyledon,* that form rosettes of leaves. Be aware that these are prone to rotting if allowed to become wet and hold water.

The soil may be surfaced with a ½in-deep mulch of washed coarse horticultural grit. This will deter weeds and keep the collars of the plants dry during winter.

Select miniature alpines and species that are not rampant. Strong-growing plants, such as *Helianthemum* (rock rose), are suitable only for large rock areas where they can spread without smothering neighboring plants.

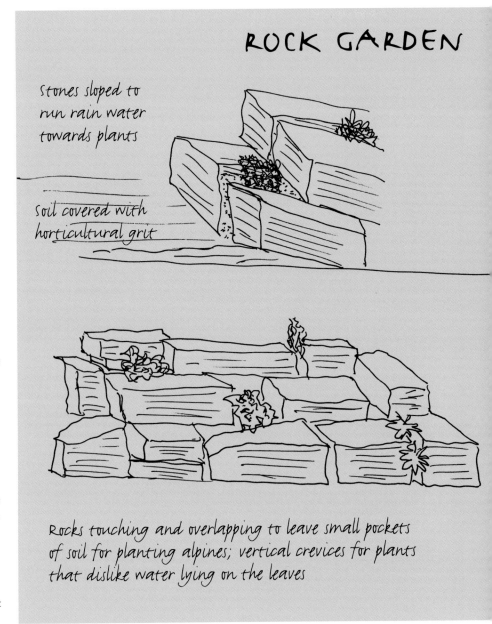

ROCK GARDEN

Stones sloped to run rain water towards plants

Soil covered with horticultural grit

Rocks touching and overlapping to leave small pockets of soil for planting alpines; vertical crevices for plants that dislike water lying on the leaves

# Mounding or banking

This is a good way to use up unwanted hard fill and poor-quality soil without the need to transport it off site: you can use it to increase the available planting surface—and when properly planted it becomes a much talked-about feature. A mound will also help to screen part of the garden and provide a windbreak for tender plants. Where the bank can be designed to run east-west, plants that enjoy full sun, such as *Helianthemum* (rock rose), *Cistus* (sun rose) and strawberries, may be grown on the south-facing slope, and moisture- and shade-loving plants, such as primroses and candelabra primulas, can enjoy the cool north side.

The width at the base of the mound should be at least half the height to the top. Use hardcore rubble in the base, followed by a layer of clay or subsoil. Cover the sunny south or west side with good-quality, free-draining topsoil. The opposite, cooler, north or east bank may be built up with old lawn sod laid upside-down or blocks of sod cut from a boggy site. Anyone turning a corner to come behind the mound will enjoy seeing a completely different type of planting.

# Pergola

There are gardens where the only opportunity for privacy is provided by a pergola. Like a patio or deck, it needn't be large; indeed, erecting a pergola over either of these two sitting areas means no additional space is taken up.

It needs to be made to a height that allows you and your visitors to stand upright, with enough space for plants to be trained across the rafters. In really small gardens, a structure 7–8ft high can look out of place or even ugly. Use a few bamboo canes to give yourself an idea of how the finished pergola will look. Traditionally, the pergola was made of timber, and while metal frames are available, to me the sturdy timber uprights and cross beams look more natural in the garden.

Where the pergola backs on to a wall, it will save timber and expense to fix a horizontal timber beam directly on to the wall and secure one end of the cross bars to it, with the other end attached to a matching beam supported on two timber uprights. Always use treated timber.

If the beams are 15in apart, climbing plants will find it easy to scramble from one beam to another, providing a dense canopy of stems, leaves, and flowers.

To make it more private, you can fill the spaces between the side uprights with timber trellis panels. A few climbers, such as clematis, roses and honeysuckle, will soon clothe the sides, providing screening and fragrance. Add a few lights, a table and chairs—and your pergola is ideal for evening drinks before supper.

LEFT: *Reclaiming an overgrown bank is hard work but once stripped of vegetation, it is a useful extension to the garden.*

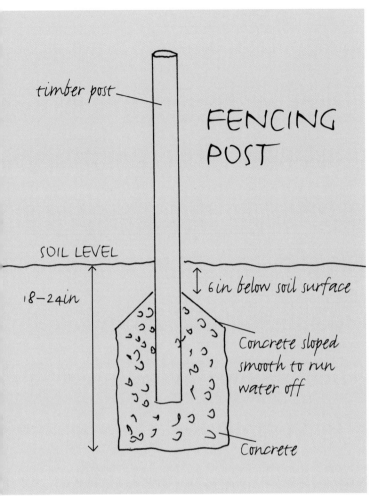

timber post

FENCING POST

SOIL LEVEL

18–24in

6in below soil surface

Concrete sloped smooth to run water off

Concrete

# Fences

Builders often use concrete posts and lines of wire to mark the boundary of the garden. This looks hideous and serves no useful purpose. It won't keep out—or in—dogs, cats, foxes, or deer. Small cottage gardens can be fenced with low picket fencing that is in keeping with the cottage effect. Vertical board fencing is strong, but is supported on runners attached to concrete posts. It looks like a fence for a public building.

Where there is a need for timber fencing to provide shelter, it should be strong and able to withstand gale-force winds pushing against it. The timber should be treated with preservative. Lightweight timber fencing and posts look ornamental, but may let you down in the first winter gale.

The bottom 18–24in of the posts should be concreted in, with the concrete 6in below soil level and smoothed and sloped with a mortar trowel to prevent water from lying beside the post.

To prevent rot, slightly raise the timber panels, leaving a 2in gap between the base and the ground. Shrubs and climbers may be grown against the panels; reserve the sunniest position for cordon-trained fruit trees.

# Clothesline

I love to see a proper clothesline carried between two posts, but the sight of clothes flapping on the line is now a rare sight in urban and even rural gardens. Unless the line is a continual loop, round pulleys, any path must be parallel and close to it. It rules out the opportunity for a curved path.

The rotary clothesline is more fashionable and practical. These lines may be folded up (but seldom are), and can be removed from the garden when not in use (but never are). The rotary line takes up less space in the garden—but tall-growing shrubs and perennials need to be planted clear of flapping sheets and shirts. It is possible to grow carpeting plants directly under the line.

# Stone trough

An authentic, old stone trough is a thing of beauty, but as a plant container it suffers from a lack of drainage. It was intended to hold water, so there is no drainage hole. With some types of stone, such as sandstone, it is possible to drill a hole in the base. Otherwise, spread a 2–3in layer of clean ½in gravel in the base, and top up with gritty, free-draining topsoil or soil mix.

A home-made trough made from an old glazed sink covered in a mixture of cement and peat will have a drainage outlet. As with other planted containers, to avoid staining the surface of the patio or deck, raise the base of the trough on flat stones or pottery "feet".

OPPOSITE: *To ensure the posts don't rot, they have been concreted in properly and capped with a lead cap.*

ABOVE: *Troughs are ideal for annuals, alpines, dwarf conifers, or bonsai trees.*

# Chapter 8— Planting, growing and nurturing your garden

It is imperative that you make yourself familiar with plants. They have their likes and dislikes, and more plants are killed every year through ignorance than through poor quality. Your garden's weather conditions and soil type will determine which plants will succeed. Knowing the final spread and planting them accordingly will prevent the bolder plants from smothering those that are dwarf or slow-growing. Where shrubs become congested, the sides that are touching lose their foliage and become misshapen.

Gardening tools and equipment, such as a spade, rake, shovel, brush, hoe, fork, trowel, and hose, will be required for initial work and planting, and also for maintenance when the garden has been laid out. Please buy the best you can afford. Cheap tools have a short life, and Murphy's Law means that they will break when they are most needed.

# Your existing garden— regenerating and recycling

Often an inherited existing garden is all wrong for the new owner. It may be an overgrown mess, or it may be a rather nice garden but just not what you want. Treat each plant according to its merit, and where a well-shaped, happy plant can't be identified, be prepared to wait a season. Some plants may be a riot of color in summer but miserable bits of bare sticks when you are appraising them. Don't throw the baby out with the bath water! One thing is certain: if you remove all the existing features, including the vegetation, the site will look much larger. This may give you false hope and make you think there is room for more than you thought. Stick to your original ideas. There will be time to change them as the design is being put into practice.

The plants that have to go should be eliminated one plant at a time, gradually to open up the area. Large unwanted plants, such as trees and shrubs, may be pruned down to stumps, and the prunings removed or chipped. The stumps may then be dug out by hand or removed with a stump grinder. Removing a single plant can often change the whole appearance of the plot. Its going gives you space, sometimes surprising you how much of the garden it previously covered. It may have been blocking sunlight and suddenly the garden is less shaded. Unfortunately, the removal of even one plant may eliminate privacy and shelter, leaving the garden or part of it exposed to the elements and in public view.

Where there are shrubs and trees that will fit into your design but are growing in the wrong place, consider lifting and transplanting them. The secret of success is not to let the plant know that it has been moved.

In the northern hemisphere, evergreens are best moved in late October or in late March when the soil is warm and rain is expected. Deciduous plants that shed their leaves in fall are best lifted after leaf fall during the period from mid-November to mid-March, providing the soil isn't frozen.

Prepare the new planting hole before lifting the plant. Make the size generous and place some well-rotted farmyard manure in the base of the pit. If there is time, fill the planting hole with water and allow it to soak away. When digging up the plant, keep well out from the trunk. A root-ball 24–30in in diameter will be adequate for most shrubs. Trees will need a root-ball at least the size of the spread of the branch canopy. Lift the plant carefully and set it on a sheet that can be tied around the ball of soil to prevent it from being shaken from the roots while the plant is being transported.

Position the plant in the hole and stand back to see how it looks. Does it look as if it belongs? Is it in proportion to the rest of the garden? Has it enough space to grow to maturity? Plant at the same depth as it was grown previously, and water well to settle the soil around the roots. Until the roots move out into the new site, some support, such as a tree stake or bamboo cane, may be necessary to prevent the plant from blowing over in a strong wind.

There are many resilient shrubs—such as escallonia, rhododendron, and yew—that will, if pruned hard, rejuvenate, producing strong new shoots from dormant buds on the stumps. If the plants have no particular sentimental value and don't appeal to you, it may be easier to start again, perhaps with better species or varieties. Shredding the unwanted plants makes their disposal easier, and the material may be used on site as wood-chip mulch. It is a particularly useful method of disposal if the only access is through the house. Shredding machines may be hired by the day.

Where there is evidence of perennial weeds, you must deal with them by digging out the roots or applying chemical weed control before your garden design is implemented on the ground. It may be difficult to remove the entire root, and with noxious weeds, such as *Convolvulus* (bindweed), leaving a single white root will allow it to re-colonize the garden. Chemicals are generally successful, but often more than one application is necessary for a total kill. Alternatively, you can cover an area infected with a perennial weed with a heavy-duty black plastic and leave it in place for an entire summer. The heat and lack of light will kill even the most persistent weed.

RIGHT: *Most shrubs and trees prefer to be planted at the same depth as previously grown.*

## SOIL

The make-up of any existing soil needs special attention. What exactly have you got and is it worth working with? Often when a small area is close to lots of buildings the ground is in awful condition, with builder's debris mixed through compacted subsoil. If you are unfortunate, just below the surface you will come across a multi-layered sheet of mortar. This is where the cement mixer was washed every time it was used and the residue allowed to harden. It needs to be broken up and removed from site.

Often the potential new garden area has been smeared with a thin skimming of topsoil which hides all the rubbish until after the house purchase is complete. Where there is good access and the area is small, the simplest solution may be to hire in an excavator and completely strip the top 8–10in for removal to a dump, then import good-quality, weed-free topsoil from a reputable source. In gardens where you are forced to work with a wheelbarrow, spade, and shovel, you will need to make do with the tools you have.

If the soil is inferior, or you have a few inches of topsoil on top of subsoil or sticky clay, one answer is to pit plant, digging generous-size holes that are filled with good soil where the plants are to be grown. Another solution is to make raised beds using good topsoil and growing above the bad.

If the existing soil is very dark— almost black—and gritty, with an absence of fiber or humus, it is probably from an old garden that has been worked and has grown plants for a very long time. First impressions may be favorable, but in reality it is a bad soil without either nutrients or fiber. There is a high

risk that it is infested with noxious weed roots and their seeds and contaminated with pests and disease spores.

By digging annual dressings of old, well-rotted, farmyard manure and compost into the top 6–8in, you can improve an inferior soil. Over a few years it will become more open, yet retentive of moisture. A balanced, general-purpose fertilizer at 60g per 3 sq ft will bulk up the nutrient level. Heavy soils may be lightened and opened up for better drainage by incorporating washed, coarse grit.

Inadequate drainage may be due to clay or compacted soil. It can cause problems and should be rectified. Where there is a suitable outlet or main drain, dig drainage channels 8in wide and 8–10in deep with a gradual fall towards the outlet to allow the water to drain away. Use 3–4in-diameter slotted plastic pipe to collect and transport the water. A covering of ½in washed gravel will filter out the soil particles and prevent the slots in the pipe from clogging. Backfill the rest of the trench with topsoil. Small areas of ground that hold puddles of water after heavy rain may simply be suffering from surface compaction. Use a digging fork to break the hard surface crust. Ease the fork up by levering the handle downwards. That may be sufficient to allow the water to percolate down through the ground.

Where there is a drainage problem but nowhere to run the water to, make a soakaway. Dig a large pit and fill it with big stones and debris to within 10in of the surface. Run the drains into this. Eventually the collected water will soak away into the subsoil. If it can be positioned directly below a patio or path, the stones may be filled to the top.

Where soil has to be removed from site, check that there is access for an excavator or, at the very least, a wheelbarrow. It may be an option to reuse the excavated material by mounding it to form the base for a rock garden or scree slope.

Excavated soil should be separated into topsoil to be retained and the subsoil that is useful only for filling and making up levels. Topsoil will usually be darker in color and easier to dig. There may be a surface layer anywhere between 4in and 12in deep. Subsoil will be hard clay or plastic-like in consistency.

## SOIL IMPROVERS

There are many ways of improving the soil, but it is as well to check its condition before you add anything. Examine the soil. Is it a heavy clay soil that remains wet in winter and bakes hard in summer? It may be sandy and free-draining. There are peat-based soils and others where there is a thin layer of topsoil over limestone or rock. (The topsoil is the dark layer; below that is the hard subsoil.) Or it may be a very dark, gritty, imported old soil devoid of nutrients and full of weed seeds and soil-borne pests and diseases.

Where you are importing topsoil for raised beds or containers, ask for a sample. Check the source and make sure that it is guaranteed free from perennial weed seeds and roots.

Adding lots of humus, such as well-rotted farmyard manure, home-made compost, or commercial leaf mould, will improve the soil, helping it retain moisture while opening it up and improving drainage.

Bagged fertilizer may be added as powder or granules. The purpose is to add beneficial nutrients to the soil that can be taken up by the plant's roots. General-purpose fertilizers are balanced, with equal parts of the main nutrients, nitrogen (N), phosphorus (P), and potassium (K). Organic fertilizers include bone meal, hoof and horn, and dried blood. Then there are slow-release fertilizers that become available to the plant's roots over 3–12 months. Liquid fertilizers have the advantage of being immediately available to the roots without having to dissolve. There are fertilizers specially designed for particular crops, such as tomatoes, roses, vegetables, and fruit.

ABOVE: *A layer of washed gravel in the base of the planting pit will assist drainage.*

ABOVE: *Digging in compost will improve the soil, opening up clay soils and helping retain moisture in sandy soils.*

## MULCHES

Applying a deep surface mulch is a particularly effective method of preventing moisture from evaporating from the ground. Soil in small raised beds and mixes in containers are prone to drying out, and a covering will keep the soil cool and retain moisture. It is therefore important that mulches are applied to moist soil and when there is still the chance of some rain.

Mulches may be used as a covering layer on top of raked soil or spread on woven membrane, such as landscape fabric, that allows the water to percolate through to the soil. The fabric prevents weeds from growing from below the mulch and is particularly useful where the weeds are tough perennials, such as bindweed or horsetail, or where the mulch is only a thin, decorative layer that won't prevent weed seeds from germinating and flourishing.

Level the surface before laying the fabric. Hollows will waste the mulch, and humps will allow the material to show through. Steep slopes are not suitable for covering with the membrane, as the layer of mulch will not be stable and will end up at the bottom of the slope. If there is a breeze, hold the fabric in place with purpose-made plastic pegs or bricks until the mulch can be spread. Overlap the sheets by 6in.

On small beds, the fabric may be laid after the plants are planted; make a slit to bring the material around each plant. It is a fiddly process—I prefer to lay the material first and using a sharp knife or scissors cut crosses where the plants are to be planted. They are planted through the fabric and, when they are firmed in, the four triangles of material are turned back to cover the soil. The mulch may then be spread over the landscape fabric.

Where the soil is known to be free of perennial weeds, you can cut a circle out of the material—or burn it out using a propane torch to melt the fabric—to aid planting. If the mulch is not at least 4in deep, weeds will grow where there is no covering of fabric close to the base of the plant.

Wood chippings are inferior to bark, but cheaper. They are an earthy brown when laid, but the wood quickly bleaches, giving the mulch a white-gray appearance. Both it and the bark tend to get scattered about during spring when birds are building new homes. Both will gradually decompose to the consistency of peat and will need to be topped up every two to three years.

Rock pieces are available in a range of often quite bright colors. They make an attractive mulch in small areas, but can be garish if used en mass. Take care that the color doesn't clash with the flowers above them.

Where the area to be mulched is small, or the plants are in containers, find a supply of pine cones to use as an interesting mulch. They are decorative and long-lasting.

RIGHT: *A layer of mulching material in containers will reduce the rate of evaporation.*
OPPOSITE: *Examples of mulching materials include gravel, bark, and wood chip.*

# How to plant

The way you plant will have an effect on the plant throughout its life. From small annuals that provide a riot of color for less than half a year to trees that will be with us throughout our lives and long after, it is the soil preparation and method of planting, along with positioning, that ensures success.

Cultivation of the soil before planting is hard work but worth doing. In large shrub beds you can avoid digging all the ground by preparing each planting pit and leaving the ground in between the plants untouched. In small areas it is simpler to do the whole lot. Again, with small areas it may not be worth the trouble of hiring a rototiller. A model powerful enough to break up hard ground will be too big for confined areas or where there is limited access.

When digging a bed by hand, use a spade with a handle long enough to feel comfortable, thus avoiding a lot of back bending. Drive the blade straight down into the soil to the full depth. As the soil is lifted, drop it forward of the hole you have made. If you work along in a straight line you will be left with a continuous trench 8–10in deep, with a mound of soil in front. Use a digging fork to break up the base of the trench, and if there is compost or old, well-rotted farmyard manure to be added, place it in the bottom of the trench.

Dig the next 6in-wide strip of soil in the same way, dropping each spadeful of soil into the trench in front, forking the new trench over and adding manure. And so on until the bed is dug over. If the ground is heavy or wet, spread a 2in layer of coarse horticultural grit on the surface

before digging. It will make standing on the soil less mucky and when dug into the ground will open up the soil and help drainage.

Where individual plant pits are being dug, each hole should be at least twice as wide as the plant roots. Where some of the subsoil has to be dug out, keep it in a separate pile from the topsoil and remove it from the site, or use it to create other features, such as a mound. Fork the base and sides of the hole to loosen hard soil. Add a layer of compost or farmyard manure to the bottom of the hole, and cover with a layer of topsoil. Both bone meal and fish, blood and bone meal are slow-acting fertilizers; 2oz (two handfuls) per plant, mixed into the topsoil as it is being backfilled around the roots, will get each plant off to a good start. If you are using home-made compost or horse manure, make sure it has heated up enough in the pile to kill weed seeds that would otherwise quickly germinate close to the plant.

Where the plant is bare-rooted, having been grown in and dug out of the ground, you must prune off any broken, damaged or dead roots. Cut them back to healthy wood, making a clean cut using sharp secateurs. Tease out tangled roots, spreading them out in the hole. Where a supporting tree stake has been driven into the hole, spread the roots to either side, keeping the stem close to it. Plant at the same depth as the plant was previously grown—there will be a soil mark on the stem. Fill the soil around the roots in layers, making sure there are no air pockets. Firm the soil with your feet. When you are satisfied that the plant is firm in the soil, dish the surface slightly towards the stem, to encourage rainwater to soak in where the roots are.

The one notable exception regarding planting depth is clematis. It is advisable to plant this at least 4in deeper than when it is in its pot. This will encourage roots to form on the buried portion of stem, reducing the risk of the plant's being killed by clematis wilt disease.

When planting container-grown plants into the ground, make sure that the roots are not tightly bundled. Where they are a tangled mass in the shape of the pot, tease out the outer roots before planting. The hole should again be twice the size of the root-ball.

The trick when re-potting container-grown plants is not to use too large a pot. Select one that is bigger than the present pot but not too large. This will encourage the roots to spread out and fill the area. If they are in a pot with lots of mix, the roots will head out to the wall of the container without making use of all the potting mix.

There are many different types of soil mixes on the market. Use ericaceous mix for plants that need acidic growing conditions. Multi-purpose mixes will suit most container-grown plants, but it is possible to buy soil-based, soil-free, and peat-free. Where weight isn't a consideration, and the plant is on a roof or balcony, I would always use a soil-based mix. It needs less watering and has the advantage of retaining nutrients and trace elements in the soil for longer. Peat-based and peat-free mixes are lighter, but tend to dry out more quickly and then are difficult to re-wet. If a pot does dry out, the secret is to plunge it in water and leave it until the root ball stops producing bubbles. Then lift it out and allow it to drain.

Where ericaceous mix or peat is being added to the planting hole, make

sure it is thoroughly wet before forking it through the soil. It is bad practice to place dry mix directly around a plant's roots. Water will run off and it will remain dry.

ABOVE: *Where the roots form a tight ball, tease them out of the mix prior to potting or planting out in the garden.*
OPPOSITE: *Make sure the planting pit is larger than the root ball.*

## HOW TO PLANT A CONTAINER

**1**

**2**

**3**

**4**

**1** Cover the drainage holes in the base of the pot with broken pieces of clay pots or lumps of styrofoam. This will prevent the soil mix from getting washed out and improve drainage. Set the pot on "feet" to lift it clear of the surface, to help water drain, and prevent pests such as ants, slugs, snails, and wood-lice from having an easy passage into the pot.

**2** Tease out tangled roots, spreading them out in the hole. Plant at the same depth as the plant was previously grown—there will be a soil mark on the stem. Fill the soil around the roots in layers, making sure there are no air pockets.

**3** Finish the soil mix at least 2in below the rim of the pot to make applying water easier and allow for a decorative mulch. The following year, a fresh layer of soil mix can be added.

**4** Firm the soil mix and water to settle it around the roots.

## NUTRIENTS

An annual application of a general-purpose granular fertilizer applied in late spring will encourage sturdy growth. Where the beds are small it is all too easy to overdose with fertilizer: 1oz or a handful per 3sq ft is adequate.

Where necessary, particular nutrients can be applied to cater for a plant's needs. Nitrogen will encourage growth and is essential for leafy plants. Extra potash will produce strong, hardy growth that is more tolerant of frost.

## SUPPORT

Trees and shrubs that are planted at a small size will usually establish without needing support. Larger plants may require a timber stake along with rubber ties and pads or a bamboo cane.

Always use a short stake that supports the lower part of the trunk but allows some movement higher up. This will strengthen the stem and encourage the roots to spread outwards. Keep a check on the plant as, with luck, after a season or two the plant will stand on its own and the stake can be removed. In the meantime, adjust the strap to allow the girth of the trunk to expand without being strangled by the tie.

Climbers and trained fruit trees will benefit from support to clamber up. Plastic or wire mesh will allow climbers such as clematis to get a grip and hold on. Horizontal wires strained to vine eyes drilled into the wall or timber panels will provide support for wisteria or vines, along with stiff-branched fruit trees such as cordon apples or espalier-trained pears. The vine eyes will hold the wires out from the vertical surface, allowing stems to twine around and leave space for tying material to be slipped between the stem and the wall.

Obelisk-shaped timber structures may be placed around the small garden to give height without spread. They are ideal for annuals such as sweet pea, *Thunbergia alata* (black-eyed Susan), and runner beans to provide maximum flower-color impact during summer.

Where there is an existing old tree or hedge, it may be used as support for other plants. Climbers, such as clematis, honeysuckle, and rambling roses, will happily scramble through their host, adding color and interest.

RIGHT: *Drill and plug the wall for vine eyes that will support training wires.*

## PLANT SPACING

It is all very well marking plants on a piece of paper drawn to scale, but when it comes to positioning them on the ground you can see better how they will look. If you know your plants and their growing habits, you will have a feel for the amount of space they require. If that knowledge is hazy, check each plant in a good reference book before placing it in the bed or border. Everyone remembers to check the ultimate height of the plant, but usually the potential spread is ignored—to the detriment of the plants.

When you buy a *Buddleja* in winter, it will have 3–4 stems, probably 2ft tall. There is nothing obvious to suggest that within one growing season that plant will be 9ft high, and more importantly, will have a spread of 4.5–6ft. Within two years it may have a height and spread of 9ft. When you plant a group of three shrubs with similar growth habits—such as *Buddleja,* forsythia, and *Philadelphus* (mock orange)—they need to be spaced 9ft apart, and they immediately look silly with all that space between them. Even in small beds, shrubs with a 3ft spread need to be spaced at least 3ft apart.

One solution is to interplant with cheap and cheerful perennials or ground-covering plants—I know there is no such thing as cheap, but let's say cheaper than the principal plants needed for the design. The idea is temporarily to fill the gaps between the permanent plants with short-term plants that may be sacrificed as they are smothered by the others. Alternatively, when the gaps have become small and before the fillers are smothered they may be dug out and, where there is space, be repositioned, given to friends, or sold at the school fair.

My favorite gap-fillers are *Kniphofia* (red hot pokers) and *Agapanthus* (African lilies). The spikes of "pokers" and blue spheres of the Agapanthus are tall enough to poke through the canopy of shrubby foliage even after they have been crowded out by the spreading shrubs. Left to fend for themselves, the stop-gap plants will eventually be smothered, but without the permanent planting being harmed. Where the main permanent planting is a selection of deciduous shrubs, the underplanting will survive for longer than when it's between evergreen shrubs and conifers.

Ground-covering plants, such as *Helianthemum* (rock rose), *Erica* (heather), *Gaultheria procumbens* (wintergreen), *Ajuga* (bugle), *Hypericum calycinum* (Rose of Sharon), and *Vinca* (periwinkle), may be used in the same way. They will carpet the bare surface until the maturing, main planting takes over.

Bedding annuals will serve the same purpose, although it is expensive to replace them twice a year, which you'll have to do as you'll be relying on pansies and polyanthus for the winter show. They may be sown under cover and transplanted out or, from May onwards, sown directly in the ground where they are to flower.

Prepare the ground between the permanent plants, raking it to make a fine surface free of large stones. Sow the seed thinly and gently rake it in, using short strokes to prevent the seed from scattering. After germination, thin the seedlings as necessary and remove any seedling weeds. Using different varieties of annuals you can get a "patchwork quilt" effect.

ABOVE: *Mark out the bed and set out the plants. Check the spacing to suit the spread of each plant.*

# Pruning

I never head out into the garden empty-handed. Invariably I carry a pair of secateurs, and I seldom return without having found something in need of a prune. It may be a broken branch, a shoot heading in the wrong direction, or a dead flower wanting to be removed.

It is possible to have a reasonable number of shrubs without having to do any regular pruning. Providing they are given sufficient space to grow, camellias, magnolias, rhododendrons, lilac, and many other common shrubs can do without any cutting for at least a decade.

A good rule of pruning is to remove the three Ds: dead, diseased, and damaged branches. That makes sense—and you should also remove branches that are growing towards the center of the plant. They cause congestion, block light, spoil the plant shape, and make future pruning difficult.

Pruning equipment must be kept sharp and clean. Ragged cuts won't heal over, which allows disease spores to enter through the cuts. Dirty blades will carry diseases from one plant to the next. Where diseased branches, such as those with canker or virus, are removed, the prunings must be collected and disposed of. Don't shred them or put them on the compost heap. Remember that pruning promotes growth, and while constant snipping is fine for a hedge, with other plants it simply builds up a mass of shoots, making them bulky.

Shrubs, such as *Philadelphus* (mock orange), that flower in summer or fall on growths made that year are pruned after flowering in winter or early spring. However, those such as forsythia, that flower in spring, on shoots produced the previous summer, are pruned immediately after flowering has finished. To prevent dieback disease, always prune young shoots immediately above a bud or side-shoot. Cherries—both ornamental and fruiting—and plums should be pruned in summer rather than in winter. During July, in the northern hemisphere, there is less risk of disease spores entering through the pruning cuts. Always look at where you are making the cut, and prune to a bud pointing in the direction you wish a new shoot to grow; the new shoot will head that way to fill a gap or replace an old branch that has been removed.

# Weeds

Weeds are the constant enemy of the gardener, and the bad news is that in a small garden it takes less time for weeds to take over. The very good news is that it takes less effort to weed a small area—and also to keep it weeded. Well-cultivated soil with a crumbly, friable surface is prone to weeds, but they are easier to remove by the root.

To my mind, there are two types of weed: those that are easily controlled and those that are not. Annual weeds are plants that germinate from seed in spring and throughout the growing season. They do not reproduce by root, and if they are constantly removed and composted before they flower and set seed, gradually the population of weeds is reduced. Unfortunately the seed may remain viable for long periods in the soil, germinating years later when the soil is cultivated. These weeds are best controlled by hand weeding; remove the whole plant with the roots attached. When the ground is wet or the soil heavy, it is best left until conditions improve. During periods of dry weather, the hoe will loosen them in the soil and allow the roots to wither and die in the sun.

Perennial weeds are the bane of the gardener's life. Once established, they are difficult to control and almost impossible to eradicate. Personally, I use chemical weedkillers such as those based on glyphosate. Applied carefully they offer the best control for a mixed collection of weeds. The chemical enters through the foliage, traveling down to the roots. Eventually the plant leaves turn yellow. Sometimes a single application will be enough to kill the weed, but more often several applications will be required to weaken the weeds and eventually kill them.

Chemical weedkillers have their limitations. They are no use to the organic gardener and are tricky to use in areas where there are other nearby plants. They may be applied only when rain isn't expected for at least 3–4 hours. Take care to apply the chemical only during calm weather, as spray drift will kill all green-leaved plants, including nearby shrubs.

Organic growers may find that covering the area for a couple of seasons with old carpet will exclude the daylight from the foliage, preventing photosynthesis from taking place, so that eventually the weeds die.

Constant removal of the foliage by hoeing achieves the same result but, with some weeds, such as horsetail and Japanese knotweed, the process is likely to take years or decades. Where the weeds are traveling through from a neighboring garden, dig a 12in-deep trench 8in wide. Line the side with a sheet of plastic held vertically up the side and protruding 2in clear of the soil surface. This barrier will prevent the neighbor's weed roots from escaping into your garden. Backfill the trench with the soil or, where the soil is heavy and wet, use washed gravel and form a drain.

Where there is no existing soil—as is often the case in basement or rooftop gardens—providing that sterilized topsoil or bagged soil mix has been used for planting, a weed problem will occur only if weed seeds blow in from surrounding gardens. (And they will.)

LEFT: *Hand weeding is a satisfactory method of removing annual weeds.*
OPPOSITE, LEFT: *Prune out and remove diseased rose stems and old shoots.*
OPPOSITE, RIGHT: *Prune above a bud pointing in the direction you want the shoot to grow.*

# Planting a lawn

Where you are sowing grass seed, the ground needs to be well cultivated and leveled, with stones larger than 1¾in in diameter removed. Do consult a specialist lawn-seed supplier for the mixture that will suit your site. There are different grasses that will tolerate shade, wet, or dry conditions. Firm the soil and sow the seed uniformly at 1.5oz per 3sq ft. Rake the seed into the top ½in of soil, and if the weather remains dry, water using a spray nozzle. Make sure you thoroughly wet the soil, as simply damping the surface may encourage germination followed by the soil's drying out and killing the seedlings.

The best time to sow grass is either in spring, when the soil is in good condition and warming up, or in the fall, while there is heat in the ground. It will be 6–8 weeks before the grass is thick enough for playing on.

A quicker route to a usable lawn is to prepare the soil in the same way but then lay bought sod that is rolled out like a carpet. Keep the sods tight together with no gaps. Water after laying, and continue to apply water during dry periods for the first season. After 5–7 days, the new lawn may be walked on and grass-cutting begun.

## HOW TO SOW A LAWN

1 A final rake before sowing. Remove debris and stones larger than 1in.

2 Sow the grass seed uniformly over the surface at 1.5oz per 3sq ft.

3 Using short strokes, rake the seed into the soil.

# Dealing with big and small pests and diseases

Even urban and city-center gardens are not immune to larger wild animals, such as deer, skunk, squirrels, and birds—especially pigeons. Then there are neighboring dogs and cats. It is difficult to fence most of them, especially deer, out. Deer or elk (depending on where you live) can be the most destructive pests of all. They are almost impossible to keep out and none of the deterrents seem to be effective for long. They are especially bad in winter, when other food is in short supply.

If your small garden is on a balcony or rooftop, your list of big-problem pests will be confined to squirrels, cats, and pigeons. Birds are interested mainly in green vegetable leaves, such as those of the brassicas—although some of our feathered friends will play havoc shredding the flowers of daffodils, pansies, and polyanthus. Occasionally finches can devour every fruit bud on apple, pear, plum, and cherry trees. One method of protection is to net the bushes.

Traditional garden pests, such as aphids, slugs, snails, vine weevils, leatherjackets, and lily beetles, are perceived to be even more troublesome in the small garden. Every attack and the damage caused will be noticed—but the good news is that there should be fewer of them to do battle with, and the battlefield is smaller.

Again, gardening on a roof or an above-ground balcony limits the numbers of pests that you have to deal with. Even snails become weary before they can climb all the way up the wall of a four- or five-story building. Greenfly may be carried upwards on air currents, but you just have to hope birds will have a meal in flight. The secret of success with these high-rise gardens is making sure that you don't bring pests, such as leatherjackets, slugs, and vine weevils, in with the soil, or greenfly, lily beetles, and leaf miners on the new plants. I have no idea how high the cabbage white butterfly can fly, but do keep an eye out for caterpillar attacks on brassica leaves.

On a small scale, the simplest control is to remove the pests by hand, making sure they can't come back. Organic soft soap may be used in the fight against some pests, such as aphids, and providing you tackle them before they multiply, the control can be excellent.

LEFT: *Pigeons are much larger and much more destructive to cabbage plants than the cabbage white butterfly.*

Diseases, such as mildew, blackspot, dieback, virus, canker, and rust, can be disastrous in a small enclosed garden. Where the garden is sheltered and the plants are close together, the conditions are ideal for rapid spread of fungal spores.

I am reluctant to use chemicals to control diseases. I am not an organic gardener, but I find many of the products are of limited use and do little to stop an attack. Prevention is better than cure, and careful examination of plants before you buy them will mean you can eliminate those with disease present. Quick action to dump those that do become diseased will often prevent spread of fungus spores. Distorted, mottled, or yellow foliage may point to virus disease; plants showing these symptoms should be isolated and if they deteriorate should be disposed of.

Occasionally, a plant dies and there is no apparent pest or disease attack. The soil may be ideal, with the plant well grown and looked after. It happens. When it does, remove the plant and have a look at the roots to see if they are healthy. If there is no evidence of decay, disease, or pest damage, dump the plant, buy something to fill the gap and carry on gardening.

Never accept plants from a friend's garden without making sure they are free of pests and diseases and appear to be growing well. Also check that they are not vigorous, weed-like plants that are hard to control.

Left: *Avoid poisoning slugs or snails where they are likely to be eaten by birds or small animals.*

# Identifying and controlling pests and diseases

*Greenfly spread diseases such as virus.*

*Caterpillars are particularly damaging to brassicas.*

*Nibbled leaf margins may be caused by vine weevil.*

## PESTS

### Aphids

These are the most common of the pests and are to be found in every garden. Most species are green, but they may also be black, pink, or yellowish. They will attack most plants, especially annuals, perennials, vegetables, and the new, young, soft tips of shrubs and trees. Some, such as the lupin aphid, are specific to a particular plant, while others will settle and suck the foliage of almost any young growth. On a small scale, the most effective control is to rub them off with your fingers. Birds and ladybugs are good predators, helping to reduce the numbers. Aphids are a nuisance when they fall from above in an arbor or pergola.

### Scale insects

These are usually seen as flattish insects covered with a waxy shell or scale and firmly stuck to the underside of leaves or stems. Young scale insects do crawl about. They suck the plant sap, weakening it and causing yellowing of the foliage. Both scale insects and aphids secrete a sticky substance called honeydew, which covers lower leaves, turning black and forming a sooty mould. Soft soap is the best control.

### Caterpillars

Caterpillars of butterflies, such as the cabbage white, and of moths, such as tortrix and codling moth, attack ornamental plants, fruit, and vegetables.

The best form of control is to destroy the eggs and pick off the caterpillars, or spray with *Bacillus Thuringiensis* (Bt). If your garden is above the seventh floor, you are unlikely to be troubled by visiting butterflies or moths.

### Spider mites

These are extremely small, resembling reddish-fawn pepper on the leaves. They suck the sap, yellowing and mottling the leaves. Their fine webbing will cover the plant. Outside, they attack peaches, strawberries, primroses, and bougainvilleas. They prefer a hot, dry climate; damping and spraying the plants deters an attack. Unless you introduce them to your rooftop or balcony garden on plants, they won't be a serious problem. Check new plants carefully and, as a precaution, drench with soft soap.

### Slugs and snails

There is no single description to cover slugs and snails. They come in all shapes, sizes, and colors, and even the shells of snails are varied. Slugs prefer acid soils, while snails are more common on alkaline (limy) ground. All plants are susceptible, and these pests will eat every stage, from seedlings to mature plants, along with soft bark and fruit. Examine plants and compost before bringing them into the garden. Snails will climb walls, so smear a deterrent along the tops of back-yard walls.

There are many ways to reduce the populations of both, and hunting them at night with a torch is effective. Looking under stones and foliage during the day will catch them unawares. Trapping is the most organic method. Baits include beer, milk, citrus peel, and bran meal—but while you will win many battles, I fear you will lose the war.

### Vine weevils

These dirty, white grubs eat bulbs, soft stems and the roots of many plants, especially those of primulas. The small black adult beetles devour foliage, eating the edges of the leaves and leaving them notched. There is a nematodal control and chemical that may be mixed into compost. Search for the beetles at night using a torch. Where your garden is all hard surface and everything is grown in containers, the best control is to be vigilant and examine all plants and the soil mix before buying.

### Leatherjackets

These are the legless, brown-gray larvae of crane fly (daddy-long-legs) that appear to have no head and that live in the ground. If you have visiting crane fly, you will probably have an attack of leatherjackets. They devour the roots of grass, leaving lawns with yellow patches during summer. They also attack vegetables and young plants. The best control is to water the lawn in the evening and cover the area with black polyethylene. Early in the morning, remove the cover. The leatherjackets will have come to the surface and may be swept up or left as bird food.

### Whitefly

These small white flies attack tomatoes, cabbages, and nasturtiums, as well as lots of indoor crops. They are sap-sucking and, when disturbed, fly around in clouds. The honeydew they secrete falls on lower foliage and goes mouldy, turning black. Catch them on bright yellow, sticky lures.

### Lily beetles

These bright red beetles have black heads, and appear on fritillaries and lilies early in spring. By midsummer the orange-red larval stage is also feeding on the foliage and flowers. On a small scale the best control is to pick off the beetles and grubs by hand. Unless they are brought in on plants, above ground, gardens will be lily-beetle-free zones.

### Capsid

The bright green capsids jump about and are seldom seen. They damage foliage and young shoots of annuals, perennials—especially chrysanthemums—and shrubs by leaving ragged-edged, small holes in leaves and in the tips of shoots. As a damaged leaf expands, the hole becomes larger. Usually, the damage is limited, but if you see a capsid you should squeeze it between your fingers.

*Typical dieback on a rose shoot.*

## DISEASES

### Virus

Virus-infected plants are common, the disease often manifesting as streaked or blotched foliage, weak growth, or stunted and distorted shoots. The disease is spread by insects, such as aphids, or through the soil. Most plants are open to attack. The best control is to dig up and destroy infected plants, and after contact with them avoid handling or pruning other plants. Don't propagate from plants showing virus symptoms.

### Dieback

The dieback fungus will often enter the plant through pruning wounds, causing the stems to become blotched, turning brown, with the leaves yellowing and falling off. Plants under stress are also more prone to attack. The dieback moves down the stem and may eventually kill the whole plant. It is a serious problem with roses and maples. The best control is to prune off infected stems, cutting well below where the disease is evident.

*Black spot disease on rose foliage.*

*Powdery mildew on a chard leaf.*

*Leaves infected with rust disease should be destroyed.*

### Canker

These fungus or bacterial diseases attack many plants, especially fruit trees, cotoneaster, and ash. There are many forms, but they are often specific to a particular host plant. The stems show dark brown or reddish-brown blotches, and the bark becomes sunken or raised and cracked. Where the canker encircles the branch, the growth above that point dies. The control is to cut out and burn all infected stems. Make the cuts at least 2–3in below the infection.

### Silver leaf

This fungal disease causes leaves to take on a silvery appearance by causing the upper and lower leaf surfaces to separate. Infected branches with a diameter larger than 1in will show a discolored ring in the cut stem. Plums and cherry trees are most susceptible. There is no control, but pruning in summer rather than in winter reduces the risk of attack through open wounds. Prune out infected branches and burn or put in the trash. The disease is not carried in the leaves.

### Rose blackspot

This is caused by a fungus, and generally appears as purple-black spots on the foliage and blotches on the stems. The leaves turn yellow and fall. In bad infections, the plant will be completely defoliated and become weakened. There are chemical controls that have some effect, but some rose varieties are more prone to attack than others. Removing infected leaves as they appear and pruning out infected stems will be of some help in preventing its spread.

### Powdery mildew

This form of mildew is more evident during hot, dry summers. It forms a white powdery coating on leaves, shoot tips, and flower buds. Particular strains will affect roses, cucumbers, brassicas, apples, gooseberries, and peas, but most plants can be attacked. There is little by way of organic control. Avoid planting in full sun, such as against a south-facing wall. Pick off young shoots as they become affected.

### Rust

Various strains of this fungal disease attack many plants, in particular roses and hollyhocks. It appears as bright orange spots on the upper leaves and orange powder-like spores on the undersides. It may cause some defoliation in early summer, but in late summer a secondary attack, when brown winter spores form on the undersides, causes total defoliation. To control the disease, spray with a fungicide. Prune out all infected stems as soon as they are seen—and destroy the prunings.

# Appendix—Plant directory

# Trees and shrubs

**Abies balsamea 'Nana':** A dwarf, evergreen selection of the balsam fir with dark green foliage. The brown winter buds open in late spring to soft, bright green shoots. It forms a rounded conifer, 3ft in height, with a similar spread. It is hardy, preferring a slightly acid soil in full sun or light shade. Providing the soil mix is kept moist, it will do well in a container. Zones 3–6

**Abutilon megapotamicum:** Evergreen or semi-evergreen shrub with thin, arching stems and bright green leaves. The pendant, bell-shaped flowers have bright yellow petals and purple stamens, surrounded by red calyces, and appear in summer and fall on the young shoots. Height and spread 6ft. Requires shelter from cold winds. Does best in fertile, well-drained soil in full sun or against a sunny wall. Zones 8–10

**Acer palmatum 'Chitoseyama':** Deciduous Japanese maple with deeply divided lobed leaves, which are an attractive pale green-red in summer, turning in early fall to a rich purple-red. It grows to 6ft in height with a 6–9ft spread, slowly forming an attractive mound. Will suffer from dieback where exposed to biting cold winds or late spring frosts. Suitable for growing in a container. Grow in a moist but well-drained soil in sun or light shade. Zones 8–10

**Akebia quinata:** Semi-evergreen climber, sometimes called the chocolate vine. The dark green leaflets are notched at the tip and blue-green on the underside, turning bronze in winter. The 4in-long, pendant clusters of brown-purple, fragrant flowers appear in early spring, followed by fleshy, purple, sausage-shaped fruit. A vigorous plant growing to 30ft, but may be kept smaller by annual pruning after flowering. Late frosts may damage the flowers. Prefers a well-drained, fertile soil in full sun. Zones 5–9

**Aloysia triphylla (lemon verbena):** Deciduous shrub with lance-shaped, lemon-scented, bright yellow leaves and tiny, pale lilac or white flowers in late summer. Height and spread 10ft. Plant in a sheltered, sunny position or grow in a container and protect in winter. Plant in well-drained, infertile, gritty soil in full sun. Zones 8–11

**Arbutus unedo 'Elfin King' (strawberry tree):** Deciduous, shrubby tree with shredding, red-brown bark and glossy, mid-green leaves. Clusters of urn-shaped white or pink-flushed flowers appear in fall, followed the following fall by spherical, warty, red fruit, with flowers and fruit on display at the same time. This is a compact variety, growing to 6ft with a 5ft spread, making it ideal for the small garden. Hardy, but for the first few seasons prone to late spring frost damage. Prefers a well-drained soil in full sun and sheltered from cold winds. Zones 8–9

**Ardisia crispa:** Evergreen shrub with leathery, dark green leaves. The clusters of small, star-shaped pink flowers appear in summer, followed by red berries. Height 3–5ft, spread 2ft. It prefers a sheltered, shaded site in a moist, well-drained, fertile soil. Can be grown in a container for color on the patio. Zones 10–12

TOP: *Acer palmatum 'Chitoseyama'*.
BOTTOM: *Akebia quinata*.

***Azara dentata:*** Arching, evergreen shrub or small tree with glossy, dark green leaves hairy on the underside. The intensely fragrant, dark yellow flowers appear in late spring. Height and spread 9ft. Plant in moist, humus-rich, fertile soil against a sunny, sheltered wall. A wonderfully perfumed plant to place a garden seat under. Zones 8–10

***Berberis linearifolia*** **'Orange King':** Evergreen shrub with arching branches of glossy, dark green, spiny leaves and clusters of orange-yellow flowers in late spring, followed by small, blue-black fruit. Height and spread 8ft. Not fussy regarding soil type, and succeeds in sun or light shade. Ideal as a spiny perimeter barrier hedge. Zones 6–9

***Brugmansia aurea*** **(angel's trumpet):** Evergreen tree or bushy shrub with bright green 6–10in-long leaves. The trumpet-shaped, golden yellow or white flowers hang down and are produced in summer and fall. They exude a powerful fragrance in the evening. Height 6–9ft in northern gardens. Where not hardy, will need to be grown in a container and kept frost-free in the winter and early spring. A superb plant for the patio, especially on a summer's evening. Zones 10–12

***Buddleja davidii*** **'Glasnevin' (butterfly bush):** Semi-evergreen shrub with dark green leaves white-woolly on the underside. The dense panicles of small, fragrant, dark lilac-pink flowers are produced from late summer to fall. Height 8ft, spread 9ft. Prefers a fertile, well-drained soil in full sun. Makes a large shrub, but needs to be pruned each spring to within 2in of the older wood. A great plant for attracting butterflies. Zones 6–9

**Buxus sempervirens 'Suffruticosa' (box):**
Evergreen shrub with small, glossy, dark green leaves. It is slow-growing, making a compact plant 3ft high with a 5ft spread. Prefers a fertile, well-drained soil in light shade. Box may be clipped hard, so is ideal as a dwarf hedge for a knot garden, along a path or as a surround to beds of vegetables. It is a favorite hiding place for snails; regular evening checks will greatly reduce their numbers. Zones 6–8

**Callicarpa bodinieri var. giraldii 'Profusion' (beautyberry):** Deciduous shrub with bronze young leaves turning dark green in early summer. The pale pink flowers appear in midsummer, followed by dark, metallic, violet fruit. Height 8ft, spread 6ft. Prefers a sheltered, sunny position in fertile, well-drained soil. Zones 5–8

**Callistemon citrinus 'Firebrand' (bottlebrush):** Evergreen shrub with arching branches and dark green leaves opening from silvery-pink young shoots. The bright crimson bottlebrush-shaped flowers appear in late spring and summer. Height and spread 5–6ft. Will thrive in a sheltered, sunny position. Prefers a moist, well-drained, fertile, neutral or acid soil in full sun. Can be trained against a sunny, warm wall. Zones 10–12

**Calluna vulgaris 'County Wicklow' (heather, ling):** Evergreen, compact-growing shrub with small, mid-green leaves and 8in spikes of pale pink flowers in late summer and fall. Height 10in, spread 16in. Requires an acid soil, preferably humus-rich and well-drained. *Calluna* varieties love the "wind in their hair", so are ideal for exposed balconies and rooftop gardens. Zones 4–7

**Camellia x williamsii 'Anticipation':**
Evergreen shrub with stiff, upright branches and glossy, bright green leaves. The large, fully double crimson flowers appear in late winter and early spring. Height 13ft, spread 6ft. Early-morning sun after a frost will damage the flowers. Prefers a sheltered, shaded position. Plant in an acid, humus-rich, well-drained soil. Will do well in a container. Zones 7–8

**Ceanothus 'Blue Mound' (California lilac):**
Evergreen shrub with small, glossy, dark green leaves and clusters of dark blue flowers in late spring. Height 5ft, spread 6ft. Prefers a sunny site sheltered from cold winds. Plant in well-drained, fertile soil. Forms a compact mound and needs its space to prevent the leaves from browning. Zones 9–10

**Chaenomeles x superba 'Crimson and Gold' (Japanese quince):** Deciduous shrub with spiny stems and glossy, mid-green leaves. The dark red flowers with bright yellow anthers appear in spring and early summer, followed by ridiculously hard green fruit that ripen yellow. Height 3ft, spread 6ft. Grow in well-drained, moist soil in full sun. Will tolerate light shade, but flowering will be reduced. Ideal for growing against a sunless wall. Zones 5–9

**Choisya arizonica (Mexican orange blossom):** Evergreen shrub with warty shoots and dark green, aromatic leaves. The pink-tinged, slightly fragrant white flowers appear in late spring. Height and spread 3ft. Benefits from a sunny, sheltered wall in well-drained soil. Zones 9–10

**Cistus x corbariensis (rock rose, sun rose):** Evergreen, bushy shrub with wavy-margined, dark green leaves. During

TOP: *Berberis linearifolia 'Orange King'*.
BOTTOM: *Callicarpa bodinieri var. giraldii 'Profusion' (beautyberry)*.
OPPOSITE: *Buddleja davidii 'Glasnevin' (butterfly bush)*.

late spring and summer the red flower buds open to pure white flowers with golden yellow centers. Height 3ft, spread 4ft. Will succeed in a sheltered site in full sun. Requires a well-drained, gritty soil. Not a long-lived plant, but ideal for a Mediterranean-type, dry garden. Zones 8–10

***Clematis alpina*** **'Frances Rivis':** Early-flowering deciduous climber with pale gray-green leaves. The petals of the single, bell-shaped, sky-blue flowers are slightly twisted. They appear in spring and early summer, followed by fluffy, silvery seed heads in fall. Height 6–9ft, spread 6ft. Dislikes cold winds. Plant in humus-rich, moist, well-drained soil in full sun or light shade. A deep mulch will keep the root area cool. Well-behaved and ideal for trellis or pergola. Zones 4–9

***Clianthus puniceus*** **(lobster claw):** Evergreen shrub with dark green leaves and, in late spring and early summer, clusters of bright red, pendant flowers the shape of a lobster's claw. Height and spread 10ft with wall support. Will succeed on a sunny wall well protected from cold winds. Grow in well-drained soil with a deep fall bark mulch. Zones 7–11

***Convolvulus cneorum:*** Compact, evergreen shrub with silky, silver-green leaves and funnel-shaped white flowers with yellow centers from late spring to summer. Height 2ft, spread 3ft. Provide shelter from late frosts and cold winds. Prefers a gritty, well-drained soil in full sun. A good container plant for summer display. Zones 8–11

***Cornus alba*** **'Sibirica' (dogwood):** Deciduous shrub with bright red bark on the young shoots. The dark green leaves color

to red in fall. Height and spread 10ft, but for a compact plant and best bark color prune every stem close to the ground each spring. Plant in moist, humus-rich soil in full sun. Zones 2–8

**Cytisus battandieri (pineapple broom):** Deciduous shrub or bushy tree with silvery-gray leaves and dense, upright clusters of pineapple-scented, bright yellow flowers in mid- to late summer. Height and spread 13ft. Will do best when grown against a sheltered warm wall. Grow in fertile, very well-drained soil in full sun. Zones 7–9

**Daphne mezereum:** Deciduous shrub with gray-green leaves. The clusters of highly fragrant, purplish-pink flowers appear in late winter and early spring before the leaves appear, and are followed by red fruit. Height 4ft, spread 3ft. Grow in moist, well-drained, humus-rich soil in sun or light shade. When they are planted close to doors or open windows, the fragrance fills the room. Zones 5–8

**Disanthus cercidifolius:** Deciduous, bushy shrub with glaucous, blue-green leaves turning gold, red, and purple in fall. The spidery, rose-red, fragrant flowers are produced in fall. Height and spread 10ft. Late frost may damage new growths. Grow in well-drained, acid soil in sun or light shade. A spectacular plant for fall color. Zones 5–8

**Erica carnea 'Springwood White' (heath):** There are many species and varieties of heath; I selected this white variety for luck! Evergreen carpeting shrub with small, bright green leaves. The one-sided stems of urn-shaped white flowers appear in late winter and early spring. Height 4in, spread 18–24in. Grow in well-drained, fertile soil

in full sun. E. carnea is tolerant of alkaline soil. Zones 4–7

**Escallonia 'Pride of Donard':** Evergreen shrub with glossy, dark green leaves and clusters of cerise-red flowers in summer. Height 5ft, spread 6ft. Dislikes cold winds and late frost, so plant in a sheltered site in well-drained soil in full sun. Ideal for coastal gardens. Makes a good thick, flowering hedge. Zones 8–9

**Euonymus fortunei 'Emerald 'n' Gold':** Evergreen shrub with bright green leaves margined with gold, becoming pink-tinged in winter. Height 5ft, spread 3ft. Grow in well-drained, fertile soil in full sun. When grown against a wall, it will manage 6ft in height before arching over. Makes an attractive dwarf clipped hedge. Zones 5–9

**Exochorda x macrantha 'The Bride' (pearl bush):** Deciduous shrub with arching branches and light green leaves. The clusters of white flowers appear in late spring and early summer. Height and spread 6ft. Any well-drained soil in sun or light shade. When grown in a sheltered garden, it may be in flower as early as mid-winter. Zones 5–9

**Fagus sylvatica 'Purpurea Pendula' (purple weeping beech):** Deciduous tree with weeping branches and deep purple leaves. Height and spread 10ft. Grow in any well-drained soil in full sun. The ideal small tree for a container with festive lights for year-round display. Zones 4–7

**Fatsia japonica (Japanese aralia):** Evergreen shrub with a spreading habit that forms a rounded bush. The dark green leaves have 7–11 lobes with wavy margins and look like a many-fingered

Top: *Cytisus battandieri (pineapple broom).*
Bottom: *Exochorda x macrantha 'The Bride' (pearl bush).*
Opposite: *Convolvulus cneorum.*

TOP: *Hibiscus syriacus 'Blue Bird'.*
BOTTOM: *Lavandula stoechas (French lavender).*
OPPOSITE: *Ledum groenlandicum (Labrador tea).*

hand. Spherical heads of white flowers, in multi-headed clusters, appear in fall and are followed by black fruits. Height and spread 5–10ft. Grow in fertile, well-drained soil in sun or dappled shade, with shelter from winter winds. Zones 8–10

***Forsythia ovata* (Korean forsythia):** Deciduous shrub with dark green leaves. The single, bright yellow flowers are produced in early spring. Height 5ft, spread 6ft. Grow in moist but well-drained soil in sun or light shade. Zones 5–7

***Fothergilla gardenii* (dwarf fothergilla):** Deciduous, bushy shrub with dark green leaves turning yellow, orange and red in fall. The fragrant spikes of small white flowers appear in spring before the leaves. Height and spread 3ft. Grow in a humus-rich, acid, well-drained soil in full sun. Zones 4–8

***Hamamelis mollis* (Chinese witch hazel):** Deciduous shrub with softly hairy, mid-green leaves that turn a buttery yellow in fall. The very fragrant golden yellow flowers are spider-like or resemble thin strips of zest, appearing on the bare branches in mid- and late winter. Height 10–12ft, spread 10ft. Avoid a cold windy site. Grow in moist, well-drained, acid or neutral soil in full sun or light shade. Zones 5–9

***Hedera helix* 'Goldchild' (English ivy):** Evergreen clinging climber with small gray-green leaves with broad creamy-yellow margins. Height 3ft. Dislikes cold winds. Grow in a fertile, well-drained, humus-rich, alkaline soil in full sun. Its compact growth makes it suitable for covering low walls or railings. Zones 5–11

***Hibiscus syriacus* 'Blue Bird':** Deciduous shrub with dark green leaves and large bright blue flowers with red centers during late summer and early fall. Height 10ft, spread 6ft. Provide shelter from cold winds and late spring frost. Grow in a well-drained, neutral-to-alkaline soil in full sun. Flowers profusely in a container and suited, in summer, to a sunny balcony. Zones 5–9

***Hydrangea quercifolia* (oak-leaved hydrangea):** Deciduous shrub with deeply lobed, mid-green leaves turning bronze-purple in fall. The panicles of white fertile and sterile flowers appear in late summer and fall; the larger, sterile, outer flowers become pink-tinged with age. Height and spread 6ft. Benefits from cold-wind and spring-frost protection. Grow in well-drained, moist soil with lots of added humus, in sun or light shade. Zones 5–9

***Jasminum polyanthum* (jasmine):** Twining, evergreen climber with deep green leaves. The strongly fragrant white flowers open from pink buds in late spring and summer. Height 10ft. Will succeed in a sheltered, sunny site. Prefers fertile, well-drained soil. Zones 9–10

***Juniperus scopulorum* 'Skyrocket' (juniper):** Evergreen, columnar conifer with gray-green leaves. Height 20ft, spread 2ft. Grow in well-drained, alkaline soil in full sun or light shade. Ideal as a means of getting height without spread. Zones 3–7

***Lavandula stoechas* (French lavender):** Evergreen shrub with aromatic, gray-green leaves and spikes of fragrant, dark purple flowers with deep purple bracts on top during summer. Height and spread 2ft. Dislikes cold winds and late frosts. Grow in well-drained, gritty soil in full sun. Makes a fragrant container-grown plant for summer color. Zones 8–9

***Ledum groenlandicum* (Labrador tea):**
Bushy, evergreen shrub with dark green
leaves rusty brown on the underside. The
clusters of small white flowers appear in
late spring. Height 2.5ft, spread 3ft. Grow
in well-drained, neutral-to-acid soil in full
sun. An excellent plant for a cold exposed
site. Zones 2–6

***Lespedeza thunbergii* (bush clover):**
Deciduous subshrub with arching branches
and blue-green leaves. The pendant, purple-
pink flowers appear in fall. Height 6ft,
spread 10ft. Grow in fertile, well-drained
soil in full sun. A good choice to extend the
flowering season into fall. Zones 6–8

***Lithodora diffusa* 'Heavenly Blue':**
Evergreen, prostrate shrub with deep green
leaves and deep blue flowers during late
spring and summer. Height 8in, spread
20in. Grow in humus-rich acid soil in full
sun. Ideal for planting on top of a low wall
where it will cascade down, forming sheets
of blue. Zones 8–12

***Lonicera fragrantissima* (honeysuckle):**
Deciduous or semi-evergreen shrub with
dark green leaves, blue-green on the
underside. The pairs of very fragrant,
creamy white flowers are produced in winter
and early spring and followed by red berries.
Height and spread 6ft. Grow in well-drained
soil in full sun or light shade. Useful for
winter perfume, but produces fewer flowers
when grown against a wall. Zones 4–8

***Magnolia stellata* 'Royal Star' (star
magnolia):** Deciduous shrub with mid-green
leaves. The silky, pale pink buds open to
pure double white flowers with thin, strap-
like petals in early and mid-spring. Height
and spread 10ft. Protect from spring frosts
that may damage the flowers. Grow in

moist, humus-rich acid or slightly alkaline soil in full sun or light shade. The open habit of the branches allows ground-covering *Ajuga* (bugle) and dwarf bulbs, such as hyacinths and *Muscari* (grape hyacinth), to form a lower tier of color. Zones 5–9

**Mahonia repens 'Rotundifolia':** Evergreen shrub with sea-green, spineless leaves. The racemes of rich yellow flowers are produced in late spring, followed by blue-black berries. Height and spread 5ft. Grow in fertile, humus-rich, well-drained soil in light or deep shade. Ideal for a cold, sunless corner where it will sucker, eventually forming a clump. Zones 5–8

**Nandina domestica (heavenly bamboo):** Evergreen shrub with 3ft-long pinnate leaves that are red-purple when young and in winter. The panicles of small, star-shaped white flowers with yellow anthers are produced in summer. They are followed by bright red fruit that last throughout the winter. Height 6ft, spread 4ft. Protect from hard frost and cold winds. Grow in well-drained soil in full sun. The variety *N. d.* 'Firepower' is compact with bright red leaves growing to 18in with a spread of 2ft. Zones 6–11

**Olea europaea (olive):** Evergreen tree with leathery, gray-green leaves silvery-green on the underside. Panicles of tiny, creamy-white, fragrant flowers appear in summer, followed by green fruit that ripen to black. Height and spread 30ft. Will succeed if sheltered from late frosts and cold wind. Grow in fertile, free-draining, gritty soil in full sun. Slow-growing: suitable for the small garden and for containers. Zones 8–10

**Olea europaea 'Veronique'** is one of several new varieties of olive that are hardy enough to grow and produce fruit outside the normally olive growing regions. It is hardy to 0°F. The small evergreen leaves are silvery green. The tree is compact in habit and ideal for container growing. Zones 7–10

**Parrotia persica 'Pendula' (weeping Persian ironwood):** Deciduous tree with glossy, deep green leaves that turn yellow, orange, flame-red, and purple in fall. Clusters of tiny, spider-like red flowers appear on the bare branches in late winter and early spring. Height 5–6ft, spread 8–10ft. Flowers may be damaged by severe frosts. Grow in moist but well-drained, fertile soil in full sun. Fall leaf color will be poor in alkaline soil. Zones 4–7

**Parthenocissus henryana (Chinese Virginia creeper):** Deciduous climber with dark green leaves conspicuously veined white, turning bright red in fall. Supports itself with tendrils. Height 30ft. It prefers a sheltered, sunny position. Grow in fertile, well-drained soil in partial shade. Less vigorous than most Virginia creepers, so suitable for shaded basement walls. Zones 8–9

**Perovskia 'Blue Spire':** Deciduous subshrub with gray-white stems and aromatic silvery-gray leaves. The tall panicles of tubular, violet-blue flowers are produced in late summer and fall. Height 4ft, spread 3ft. Grow in well-drained, infertile soil in full sun. Makes a good show in a mixed border and thrives in coastal gardens. Zones 5–8

**Philadelphus 'Lemoinei' (mock orange):** Deciduous shrub with arching stems and mid-green leaves. The small, cup-shaped, pure white flowers are incredibly fragrant and are produced in racemes in early and midsummer. Height and spread 5ft. Grow in fertile, well-drained soil in sun or light shade. A single plant of *P*. 'Lemoinei' will fill a small garden with summer perfume. Zones 4–8

**Pieris formosa var. forrestii 'Jermyns':** Evergreen shrub with arching branches and deep red young leaves. The dark red flower buds open to pendant panicles of white flowers. Height and spread 7ft. Young growths may be damaged by late spring frosts or cold winds. Grow in humus-rich, well-drained, acid soil in sun or light shade. Zones 6–9

**Pittosporum tenuifolium 'Tom Thumb':** Evergreen shrub with crinkle-edged leaves that open green, turning bronze-purple. In spring the compact, rounded plant produces small, bright green leaves on top of the darker foliage. Height 3ft, spread 2ft. Prefers a sheltered position screened from cold winds. Grow in fertile, moist but well-drained soil in full sun. Zones 9–11

**Poncirus trifoliata (hardy orange):** Deciduous shrub with bright green shoots and large, very sharp spines. The dark green leaves turn yellow in fall. Saucer-shaped white, fragrant flowers appear in late spring and early summer, followed by small, orange-like, inedible green fruit that ripen to orange. Height and spread 10ft. Grow in fertile, well-drained soil in a position sheltered from cold winds and in full sun. The spines are vicious and dangerous for children. Planted under a window, it is a marvellous deterrent to burglars. Zones 5–9

**Prunus 'Amanogawa' (flowering cherry):** Deciduous tree with stiff branches forming a narrow, upright shape. The yellow-bronze

TOP: *Pieris formosa var. forrestii 'Jermyns'.*
BOTTOM: *Pittosporum tenuifolium 'Tom Thumb'.*
OPPOSITE: *Parrotia persica 'Pendula' (weeping Persian ironwood).*

Top: *Salvia greggii 'Raspberry Royal'*
*(fall sage).*
Bottom: *Salix gracilistyla 'Melanostachys'*
*(black pussy willow).*
Opposite: *Syringa x persica (Persian lilac).*

leaves become green, turning yellow, orange, and red in early fall. The clusters of semi-double, pale pink flowers appear in mid-spring and are fragrant. Height 20ft, spread 4ft, eventually spreading to 7–10ft. Grow in moist but well-drained soil in full sun. Because the stiff, upright branches don't wave about in a breeze, the flowers are less prone to being blown off. A great plant for hiding a service pole. There are many other cherries suitable for small gardens. Zones 6–8

**Pyracantha atalantioides (firethorn):** Evergreen shrub with spiny stems and glossy, dark green leaves. The clusters of white flowers appear in spring, followed by bright orange-red berries that will remain on the plant until the following spring. (Birds dislike the bitter taste.) Height 15ft, spread 12ft. Benefits from shelter from cold winds and severe frost. Grow in well-drained, fertile soil in full sun or light shade. Spectacular, especially in winter, when trained against a wall. Zones 6–9

**Rhododendron 'Princess Anne':** Semi-dwarf, evergreen shrub with young leaves opening bronze, turning mid-green by late spring. The plentiful trusses of funnel-shaped, green-tinged, primrose-yellow flowers appear in mid-spring. Height and spread 2.5–3ft. Avoid cold, exposed sites. Grow in fertile, acid, well-drained soil in full sun. There is an enormous number of dwarf, compact-growing varieties of rhododendron suitable for the small garden and ideal for growing in containers. Zones 6–8

**Rosa (rose):** These are the most loved of all the garden flowers, and choice is personal. When choosing, bear in mind size. There are miniature roses fit for a

rock garden, and compact patio roses for growing in containers. Bush roses and shrub roses are wonderful individually or planted en masse. Climbers and ramblers are ideal for walls and arches, but some are incredibly vigorous and too aggressive for the small garden. Not all roses are perfumed; where possible, smell a flower rather than relying on a catalogue description. Attacks by pests and diseases are common problems. Hardiness varies.

**Rosmarinus officinalis 'Benenden Blue' (rosemary):** Evergreen shrub with narrow, dark green, aromatic leaves. The vivid blue, tubular flowers are fragrant, appearing in the leaf axils from late spring to summer, often with another flush in fall. Height and spread 5ft. Grow in well-drained, gritty soil in full sun. A must-have culinary herb, it makes a wonderful aromatic, evergreen hedge, but has to be clipped every year after flowering. Zones 8–11

**Salix gracilistyla 'Melanostachys' (black pussy willow):** Deciduous bushy shrub with silky-hairy, gray-green leaves. It is a male variety, with black catkins and deep red anthers in early spring before the leaves appear. Height and spread 7–10ft. Grow in moist but well-drained soil in full sun. The catkins are unusual, and wonderful in a flower arrangement. Zones 5–8

**Salvia greggii 'Raspberry Royal' (fall sage):** Evergreen shrub or woody perennial with shoots from the base and leathery, mid- to deep-green leaves. The terminal racemes of paired, bright red flowers appear in late summer and fall. Height and spread 12–15in. Protect from winter wet and cold, drying winds. Grow in gritty, well-drained, humus-rich soil in full sun. Zones 7–9

***Sophora microphylla* 'Sun King':** Evergreen small tree or shrub with dark green, pinnate leaves on silky shoots. The pendant racemes of pea-like orange-yellow flowers appear in late winter and early spring, followed by long, trailing seed pods. Height and spread 10ft. Dislikes cold, drying winds. Grow in fertile, well-drained soil in full sun. Grow as a standard with a 6ft clear stem, and position a seat below the head of the tree. Zones 8–10

***Syringa* x *persica* (Persian lilac):** Deciduous, compact shrub with dark green leaves. In late spring and early summer it produces masses of small panicles of fragrant, purple flowers. Height and spread 6ft. Late spring frosts may damage new growths. Grow in humus-rich, fertile, well-drained, neutral or alkaline soil in full sun. It has a fairly light head of branches, allowing spring bulbs and carpeting plants to grow in its shadow. Zones 3–7

***Taxus baccata* 'Fastigiata Aureomarginata' (golden Irish yew):** Columnar, evergreen yew with small, dark green leaves edged with bright yellow. It is female, producing single green seeds, each surrounded by a juicy, sweet, red outer coat (aril). With the exception of the seed coat, all parts are toxic. Height (slow-growing to) 10ft, spread 3–6ft. Grow in any fertile, well-drained soil in full sun or light shade. A good dot plant to provide height. Ideal for planting between a service pole and the main viewing position. Zones 7–8

***Thuja occidentalis* 'Little Champion':** Dwarf, evergreen conifer with small, bright green leaves scented of apple. Height and spread 3ft. Shelter from cold, drying winds. Grow in moist, well-drained soil in full sun.

TOP: *Vaccinium macrocarpon (cranberry)*.
BOTTOM: *Vitis 'Brant' (grape vine)*.
OPPOSITE: *Wisteria sinensis 'Sierra Madre'*
*(Chinese wisteria)*.

Ideal as a specimen conifer for the small garden, in a container on the patio or as a matching pair positioned either side of the door or steps. Zones 2–7

**Thymus x *citriodorus* (lemon-scented thyme):** Evergreen shrub grown as a herb with small, lemon-scented, mid-green leaves and heads of pale, lavender-pink flowers in summer. Height 8–12in, spread 8in. Grow in well-drained, gritty, neutral-to-alkaline, infertile soil in full sun. May be planted as a path edging or in containers and window boxes. Zones 6–9

**Vaccinium macrocarpon (cranberry):** Evergreen shrub with dark green leaves that turn bronze in winter. Produces single or clusters of pendant, bell-shaped, pink flowers in summer, followed by edible red berries. Height 6in. If not curtailed will spread far and wide. Grow in permanently moist, acid soil in sun or light shade. Makes a good carpet under other plants, with fruit that children love. Zones 2–7

**Vinca minor 'La Grave' (periwinkle):** Evergreen, mat-forming shrub with dark green leaves. The lavender-blue flowers appear from mid-spring through to fall. Height 4–6in, spread indefinite. The trailing shoots readily root, allowing the plant to spread quickly. Grow in any soil except on ground that completely dries out in summer in full sun or shade. Will have more flowers in a sunny position. Because they are easy to propagate and spread rapidly, periwinkles get a bad press—but are ideal for covering and stabilising a steep bank. Will flower for most of the year, even supplying a few flowers most winters. Zones 4–9

**Vitis 'Brant' (grape vine):** Deciduous climber with bright green leaves turning bronze-purple in fall while retaining green veins. In late fall it produces large bunches of small, blue-black, sweet, edible fruit. Height 20–25ft. A vigorous plant, needing something to climb and scramble over. Grow in neutral-to-alkaline, well-drained, gritty soil in full sun or light shade. Where there are wires or timber support, it will, while in leaf, disguise pipework on walls or old walls in need of repair. Zones 5–9

**Weigela 'Snowflake':** Deciduous shrub with dark green leaves. The pure white, bell-shaped flowers appear in late spring and early summer. Height 4ft, spread 5ft. Grow in fertile, well-drained soil in full sun or light shade. Zones 5–9

**Wisteria sinensis 'Sierra Madre' (Chinese wisteria):** Deciduous twining climber with mid-green pinnate leaves. The foot-long, pendant racemes of pea-like, fragrant, dark lavender flowers have white-flushed standard petals, produced in late spring and early summer. They are followed by long, bean-like, soft green seed pods. Height 25ft. The flowers may be damaged by late frosts. Grow in fertile, moist but well-drained soil in full sun or light shade. Zones 5–8

**Yucca filamentosa 'Bright Edge' (Adam's needle):** Evergreen shrub with basal rosettes of lance-shaped, stiff, bright green leaves broadly margined with bright yellow. The 6ft-long, upright panicles of bell-shaped white flowers are tinged with cream or pale green and appear in late summer and fall. Height 30in, spread 4ft. Dislikes cold winds and late spring frosts. Grow in well-drained, sandy soil in full sun. May be grown in a container, providing the drainage is good. A spectacular plant guaranteed to give the impression of hotter climates. Zones 4–11

# Perennials for the small garden

TOP: *Acaena microphylla 'Copper Carpet'*.
BOTTOM: *Alchemilla mollis (lady's mantle)*.
OPPOSITE: *Carex elata 'Aurea' (Bowles' golden sedge)*.

**Acaena microphylla 'Copper Carpet':** An evergreen perennial with small, bronze, pinnate leaves and tiny, round, petalless flowers, followed in late summer by bright red burrs 1in in diameter. It is ideal for the rock garden or for edging a patio. Height 1 1/4in, spread 20in. Prefers a well-drained soil in full sun or light shade. Zones 6–8

**Aconitum 'Bressingham Spire':** Perennial with glossy, dark green leaves and racemes of deep violet-blue flowers on 3ft-high stems in summer and early fall. It forms a 1ft clump. Grow in moist, fertile soil in light shade. It is ideal for a woodland setting, and the flowers are good for cutting. Contact with the foliage may irritate the skin. Zones 3–7

**Adiantum pedatum:** A deciduous fern with lance-shaped, pinnate, mid-green fronds. The 12–16in stalks are glossy black. Forms a clump 15in in diameter. Prefers a moist but well-drained, fertile soil. Suitable for shade. Zones 3–8

**Agapanthus campanulatus:** A deciduous perennial with narrow, strap-like, grayish-green leaves and large, round heads of bell-shaped, light or dark blue flowers during summer. Height 24–36in, spread 16–18in. Grow in fertile, moist but well-drained soil in full sun. *A. africanus* is evergreen, with deep blue flowers, but needs protection from winter frosts. Ideal in a container on a sunny patio. Zones 7–10

**Ajuga reptans 'Multicolor':** A mat-forming, spreading evergreen perennial with dark bronze-green leaves blotched with pink and cream. The small, upright spikes of deep blue flowers appear in late spring and early summer. Height 6in, spread 2ft. Will tolerate poor, infertile soil and deep shade, so is ideal for growing under trees or bulky evergreen conifers or shrubs. Zones 3–9

**Alcea rosea (hollyhock):** Perennial with large, rough-surfaced, pale green leaves and 5–7ft-high spikes of flowers in early to midsummer. The single flowers may be white, yellow, pink or purple. Will require staking in windy gardens. Prefers a well-drained soil in full sun. Prone to rust disease, so often grown as a biennial. *A. rosea* 'Charter's Double' produces double flowers in a wide range of colors. Ideal against a wall or along a path for that old-world cottage look. Zones 3–9

**Alchemilla mollis (lady's mantle):** Perennial with softly hairy, pale green leaves. The masses of tiny, greenish-yellow flowers appear like froth from early summer to fall. Drops of rain look like mercury sitting in the hearts of the leaves. Remove all the foliage and dead flowers after flowering for a second flush of young leaves. Height and spread 2ft. Prefers a moist, humus-rich soil in full sun. Drought-tolerant and good for cut flowers. Zones 4–7

**Anthemis tinctoria 'E. C. Buxton':** A clump-forming deciduous perennial with mid-green base leaves and smaller leaves on the branching flower stems. Each stem carries a single, lemon-yellow, daisy-like flower head with a deep yellow 'button' center. Height 16–24in. Prefers a well-drained, gravelly soil in full sun. The blooms appear throughout the summer and fall and are excellent cut flowers. Zones 3–8

***Asplenium scolopendrium:*** An evergreen fern with strap-like, glossy, bright green and leathery fronds 16in long. It will eventually form a clump 24in in diameter. Grow in partial shade in a humus-rich, moist but well-drained, alkaline soil. Zones 6–8

***Astilbe* 'Aphrodite':** Deciduous perennial with deeply divided bronze-green leaves. The upright plumes of small, bright red flowers appear in summer. Height and spread 20–24in. Needs a humus-rich, moist soil in full sun. Ideal for a woodland planting or in a bog garden. Zones 3–8

***Bergenia* 'Baby Doll' (elephant's ears):** A clump-forming evergreen perennial with 4in-long, glossy, mid-green leaves that turn bronze-purple in late fall. The soft pink flowers appear in spring on red stalks. Height 12in, spread 18in. Prefers a sheltered site. Frost may damage the early flowers. Grows best in a moist but well-drained soil in full sun or light shade. Zones 4–8

***Campanula chamissonis* 'Superba':** Perennial with rosettes of pale green leaves. The bell-shaped, pale blue flowers appear in early summer. Height 2in, spread 8in. Needs free-draining, gritty soil. Ideal for a rockery or planted in crevices in a patio or a dry-stone wall. Zones 4–7

***Canna* 'Pfitzer's Chinese Coral' (Indian shot):** Upright perennial with gray-green leaves. The coral-pink flowers are gladiolus-like, appearing in abundance from midsummer until fall. Height 30in, spread 18in. Survives best outside in a sunny, sheltered site. Where tender, plant out after frost, or grow in pots for use on the patio. Cannas provide the wow factor as dot plants in a bedding scheme. Zones 8–11

***Carex elata* 'Aurea' (Bowles' golden sedge):** Deciduous perennial with arching yellow leaves margined with green. The brown male flower spikes appear in late spring and early summer. Height 2ft, spread 16in. Prefers well-fertilized, moist or wet soil in sun or light shade. Zones 5–9

***Centaurea macrocephala* (giant knapweed):** Deciduous perennial with 6–8in-long, rough-textured, lance-shaped, mid-green leaves, sometimes toothed, forming a clump. In mid- to late summer, leafy, upright stems carry bright yellow fluffy flower heads above brown scaly bracts. They make good cut flowers or the resulting seed pods can be dried for winter decoration. Height to 5ft, spread 2ft. Well-drained soil in full sun. Zones 3–7

***Corydalis flexuosa:*** Summer-dormant perennial with light green leaves sometimes flushed purple. The clusters of dainty tubular, bright blue flowers, each with a white throat, appear in late spring and early summer. Height 12in, spread 10in. Grow in humus-rich, well-drained soil in light shade. Zones 6–8

***Delphinium* 'Black Knight':** A perennial. One of the Pacific Hybrids usually grown as a biennial or an annual, with basal light green leaves. The tall spikes of semi-double, deep purple flowers, each with a black eye, appear in early and midsummer. Height 2ft, spread 20in. A windy site will cause damage to the flower spike. Grow in fertile, well-drained soil in a sheltered, sunny position. Zones 3–9

***Deschampsia flexuosa* (wavy hair-grass):** Evergreen perennial grass with thin, bluish-green leaves and panicles of silvery-purple spikelets during summer. Height 2ft, spread

16in. Grow in moist acid soil in full sun or light shade. Ideal for adding height to a container or as a dot plant. Zones 4–9

**Dianthus erinaceus:** Evergreen perennial with mid-green leaves forming a low cushion. The light pink, single flowers appear in summer. Height 2in, spread 16in. Prefers a well-drained, alkaline soil in full sun. Ideal for the rock garden or on the sunny side of a mound. Zones 4–9

**Dicentra spectabilis (bleeding heart, Dutchman's breeches):** Perennial with pale green leaves and arching stems of rose-pink and white flowers during late spring and early summer. Height 4ft, spread 16in. Early growth may be damaged by frost. Grow in moist, humus-rich, alkaline soil in light shade. Tolerates full sun where the soil doesn't dry out. Zones 3–9

**Dierama pulcherrimum 'Blackbird' (angel's fishing rod):** Evergreen perennial with thin, grass-like, gray-green leaves. The arching stems of bell-shaped, dark wine-purple flowers appear in summer. Height 5ft, spread 25in. Prefers a sheltered, sunny position in well-drained, humus-rich soil. Zones 8–10

**Digitalis purpurea f. albiflora (foxglove):** Biennial or short-lived perennial with a basal rosette of dark green leaves. The tall, one-sided spikes of pure white flowers are produced in early summer. Height 4ft, spread 18in. Any soil other than very dry or waterlogged. Prefers a humus-rich, moist soil in partial shade. Good as a cutting flower. Zones 4–8

**Echium pininana:** Evergreen biennial or short-lived perennial with lance-shaped, roughly hairy leaves. The tall spikes of

thousands of small, funnel-shaped blue flowers appear in mid- and late summer. Height 13–16ft, spread 30in. Protect from frost with horticultural fleece in winter. Grow in fertile, well-drained soil in full sun. Zones 9–10

**Eremurus stenophyllus (foxtail lily, desert candle):** Perennial with rosettes of foot-long basal leaves and tall stems, bare of leaves, which carry a raceme of small, star-shaped, bright yellow flowers in summer. Height 5ft, spread 2ft. Early growth is prone to frost damage. Grow in a sheltered position in open gritty, free-draining soil in full sun. A group planting among low-growing shrubs or perennials has a wow factor. Zones 4–9

**Erysimum 'Bowles' Mauve':** Evergreen perennial with lance-shaped, gray-green leaves and long racemes of mauve flowers from late winter until early fall. Height 30in, spread 20in. Grow in well-drained, neutral-to-alkaline soil in sun. Zones 6–10

**Festuca glauca:** Evergreen perennial grass with blue-green leaves. The short panicles of blue-green flowers appear in summer. Height 12in, spread 8in. Grow in dry, well-drained soil in full sun. Zones 4–8

**Gentiana acaulis (trumpet gentian):** Evergreen perennial with rosettes of glossy, dark green leaves. The solitary, trumpet-shaped deep blue flowers with green spots on the inside appear in late spring. Height 3in, spread 12in. Grow in humus-rich, well-drained soil. Where the summers are cool, plant in full sun. Zones 5–8

**Geranium maderense:** Evergreen perennial with deeply lobed, bright green leaves. The large panicles of magenta flowers with pink

Top: *Eremurus stenophyllus (foxtail lily, desert candle)*.
Bottom: *Festuca glauca*.
Opposite: *Corydalis flexuosa*.

veins and red anthers appear in late winter and early spring on stout stalks. Height and spread 4ft. Shelter from frost and cold winds. May be grown in a container. Grow in well-drained soil in full sun. Zones 8–9

*Helleborus niger* **'Potter's Wheel' (Christmas rose):** Evergreen perennial with leathery, dark green basal leaves. The large, bowl-shaped, white flowers have green centers held above the foliage on stout stems. Height 12in, spread 18in. Avoid a cold windy site. Grow in humus-rich, moisture-retentive, neutral-to-alkaline soil in light shade. Ideal for the sunless side of a mound or as a clump in the shade of a tree. Zones 4–8

*Hosta fortunei* **'Aureomarginata' (plantain lily):** A perennial with bold, deeply veined, heart-shaped, leathery, deep green leaves margined yellow. The funnel-shaped, mauve flowers appear in midsummer. Height and spread 3ft. Grow in moist, well-drained soil in sun or shade and sheltered from cold winds. Will succeed in cold, heavy gardens or in a bog garden—but watch out for slugs and snails. Zones 3–9

*Imperata cylindrica* **'Rubra':** Perennial grass with 20in-long, thin mid-green leaves that quickly become deep red. Silvery-white, fluffy panicles appear in late summer. Height 20in, spread 12in. Will succeed in a sheltered position outside with a winter mulch. Grow in moist, well-drained soil in sun or light shade. Zones 5–9

*Iris unguicularis* **(iris):** Rhizomatous perennial with grass-like evergreen leaves and single, large, fragrant, pale blue to deep violet flowers with a band of yellow, carried on short stems in winter and early spring. Height 12in. Grow in well-drained, neutral-to-alkaline soil in full sun. Ideal for the base of a dry, sunny wall. Zones 7–9

*Kniphofia* **'Strawberries and Cream' (red-hot poker):** Deciduous perennial with long, thin, dark green leaves. In late summer and fall, the cream flowers are coral-pink in bud, giving a bicolour effect. Height 2ft, spread 1ft. Grow in deep, fertile, moist but well-drained soil in full sun or shade. Zones 6–9

*Ligularia dentata* **'Desdemona' (golden groundsel):** Perennial with brownish-green leaves, deep purple-red on the underside. The deep orange, daisy-like flower heads appear in summer and early fall. Height and spread 3ft. Grow in fertile, moist soil in sun in a sheltered position. Slugs and snails love it. Zones 4–8

*Lysichiton americanus* **(yellow skunk cabbage):** Aquatic perennial with large, 20–35in-long, glossy, mid-green leaves. The enormous bright yellow spathes appear in early spring. They have a musky, almost skunk-like smell. Height and spread 3ft. Grow in humus-rich soil at the edge of a stream or pond in sun or light shade. Zones 7–9

*Meconopsis grandis* **(Himalayan blue poppy):** Deciduous perennial with rosettes of dark green leaves with rust-colored hairs. The cup-shaped, bright blue flowers with a cluster of yellow anthers are produced in early summer. Height 3ft, spread 2ft. Requires shelter from cold winds. Grow in a moist, neutral-to-acid soil with lots of added leaf mould in light shade. Tends to be monocarpic if planted in ground that dries out in summer. It helps if you prevent seed from forming for the first season. Zones 5–8

TOP: *Helleborus niger 'Potter's Wheel' (Christmas rose).*
BOTTOM: *Kniphofia 'Strawberries and Cream' (red-hot poker).*
OPPOSITE: *Phormium 'Sundowner' (New Zealand flax).*

***Miscanthus sinensis* 'Silberfeder':**
Deciduous perennial grass with arching, mid-green leaves and tall panicles of pale pink, silvery-brown flowers in fall and lasting throughout the winter. Height 8ft, spread 3ft. Grow in fertile, well-drained soil in sun. A good plant to provide height without forming a permanent screen. Zones 4–9

***Myosotidium hortensia* (Chatham Island forget-me-not):** Evergreen perennial with large, glossy, bright green leaves with prominent veins. The dense clusters of bell-shaped, dark or pale blue flowers appear in early summer. Height 2ft, spread 18in. Will succeed sheltered from cold winds. Grow in moist but well-drained soil in light shade. Enjoys an annual mulch of seaweed. Zones 10–12

***Nepeta* x *faassenii* (catmint):** Perennial with aromatic, silvery, gray-green wrinkled leaves. The clusters of lavender-blue flowers have purple spots and are produced from early summer to fall. Height and spread 15–20in. Grow in well-drained soil in full sun or light shade. Zones 4–8

***Oenothera caespitosa* (evening primrose):**
Biennial or perennial with rosettes of gray-green leaves and fragrant, cup-shaped white flowers that open in the evening during summer. As they age, the flowers turn pink. Height and spread 10in. Grow in infertile, well-drained, gritty soil in full sun. Good for evening fragrance in the garden. Zones 4–8

***Ophiopogon planiscapus* 'Nigrescens' (lilyturf):** Evergreen perennial with strap-shaped, deep purple-black leaves. The racemes of pinkish-white flowers appear in summer, followed by strings of blue-black fruit. Height 8in, spread 16in.

Top: *Ophiopogon planiscapus 'Nigrescens' (lilyturf)*.
Bottom: *Persicaria bistorta 'Superba' (bistort, knotweed)*.
Opposite: *Pennisetum villosum (feathertop)*.

Grow in fertile, well-drained, slightly acid soil in full sun or light shade. Provides a dark carpeting backdrop for spring bulbs. Zones 6–11

***Pachysandra terminalis:*** Evergreen perennial with glossy, dark green leaves and spikes of small, white male flowers in early summer. Height 8in. Will spread far and wide. Avoid very dry ground. Plant in sun or light shade. A good evergreen for ground cover where the soil is wet and shaded. Zones 4–8

***Paeonia officinalis* 'Flame' (common peony):** Herbaceous perennial with deep green leaves and single, bright rose flowers with bright yellow stamens in early and midsummer. Height and spread 2ft. Young foliage may be damaged by late frosts. Shelter from cold winds. Peonies prefer a humus-rich, moist, fertile, well-drained soil in sun or light shade. Zones 3–8

***Papaver orientale* 'Black and White' (Oriental poppy):** Perennial with white-bristly stems and mid-green leaves. The large, solitary, cup-shaped white flowers have a deep crimson-black blotch at the base of each tissue-paper-like petal; they appear from late spring to midsummer. Height 2ft, spread 18–24in. Prefers a deep, fertile, well-drained soil in full sun. A good early-summer-flowering perennial to fill short-term gaps between permanent shrubs. Zones 3–9

***Pennisetum villosum* (feathertop):** Deciduous perennial grass with arching stems of mid-green leaves. The cylindrical, plume-like panicles of flowers with their pale green bristles appear in late summer and fall and turn purple. Height and spread 20in. It is often grown as an annual.

Grow in sandy, well-drained soil in full sun. Zones 9–12

***Persicaria bistorta* 'Superba' (bistort, knotweed):** Semi-evergreen perennial with mid-green leaves and tall stems with spikes of soft pink flowers. They are produced over a long period from early summer to late fall. Height 3ft, spread 16in. Grow in sun or light shade in any soil other than waterlogged. It is tolerant of dry, shaded ground. Zones 4–8

***Phormium* 'Sundowner' (New Zealand flax):** Evergreen perennial with broad, upright, sword-like leaves that are bright bronze-green with yellow and pink stripes. The 6ft-tall panicles of greenish-yellow flowers produced in summer. Height and spread 6ft. In cold gardens prone to frost it's a good idea to provide a deep mulch of bark in late fall. Grow in moist but well-drained soil in full sun. As a hedge, it forms an impenetrable screen and will spread sideways if not curtailed. Zones 9–10

***Primula florindae* (giant cowslip):** Deciduous perennial with mid-green leaves. The mealy-white, pendant, funnel-shaped sulphur-yellow flowers are incredibly fragrant and appear in summer on tall, stout stems with up to 40 flowers per stem. Height 4ft, spread 3ft. Grow in moist, humus-rich, neutral-to-acid soil in sun or light shade. Ideal for a bog garden or a particularly wet and shady position. There are many species of primula, including primroses, polyanthus and the candelabras. Zones 3–8

***Rhodohypoxis baurii* 'Helen':** Herbaceous perennial with corm-like roots and lance-shaped, folded, greyish-green leaves. Solitary 2–2.5in-diameter white flowers are produced during summer. Height and

spread 4in. Do well in soil kept almost dry in winter. Grow in fertile, well-drained, humus-rich soil in full sun. Ideal for small containers or window boxes. Multiplies quite rapidly in a well-drained, gritty rock garden site. Zones 9–10

***Rodgersia pinnata* 'Superba':** Rhizomatous perennial with purplish-bronze young leaves becoming large and glossy, dark green. The tall panicles of small, star-shaped, bright pink flowers are produced during mid- and late summer on reddish-green stalks. Height 3ft, spread 28cm. Young leaves may be damaged by late spring frosts or cold, drying winds. Grow in humus-rich, moist soil in sun or light shade. Avoid soil that dries out in summer. Zones 3–7

***Rudbeckia fulgida* var. *sullivantii* 'Goldsturm' (black-eyed Susan):** Perennial with mid-green leaves. The large, daisy-like, golden-yellow flower heads with button-like, dark brown disc florets in the center appear from late summer to late fall. Height 2ft, spread 16in. Grow in full sun or light shade in fertile, well-drained soil that doesn't dry out in summer. Good as a cutting flower and is tolerant of heavy clay soil. Zones 4–9

***Saxifraga* 'Tumbling Waters' (saxifrage):** Evergreen perennial with large rosettes of lime-encrusted, silvery-green leaves. The large, conical panicles of small, cup-shaped white flowers appear in spring. They are slow to come into flower, often taking 2 years. Height 16in, spread 12in. Dislikes heavy rain. Grow in fertile, very well-drained, gravelly, alkaline soil in full sun. Ideal for a scree bed at the base of a rockery, or in an alpine collection in a container. Zones 6–7

***Sedum spectabile* 'Septemberglut' (ice plant):** Deciduous perennial with gray-green, thick, succulent leaves. The flat clusters of small, star-like, deep pink flowers appear in late summer. Height 20in, spread 16in. Grow in fertile, well-drained, neutral or slightly alkaline soil in full sun. The flowers are a great attraction to bees and butterflies, especially late in the season. Zones 4–9

***Tricyrtis flava* (toad lily):** Herbaceous perennial with hairy stems and mid-green leaves, often with dark purple spots. The star-shaped, upward-facing yellow flowers with purplish-brown spots are produced in fall, either singly or in clusters. Height and spread 12–16in. Grow in moist but well-drained, humus-rich soil in light or deep shade. Dislikes soil that dries out in summer. Ideal for a cool part of the garden in deep shade, adding color late in the season. Zones 6–9

***Trillium sessile* (wake-robin, toadshade)**. Deciduous perennial with stalkless, deep green leaves marbled with pale green, deep maroon and gray. In late spring the stalkless, deep red-maroon flowers with their maroon-flushed green sepals are produced above the leaves. Height 12in, spread 8in. Grow in moist, well-drained neutral-to-acid, humus-rich soil in light or deep shade. A good plant for a reliably moist soil in deep shade. In flower it is a talking point for visitors. Zones 4–8

***Tropaeolum speciosum* (flame creeper):** Perennial climber with small, mid- to dark green leaves. The bright red, long-spurred flowers appear in summer and fall, followed by spherical blue fruit with red calyces. Height 9ft. Grow in moist, humus-rich, neutral-to-acid soil with the head in full sun or light shade. It prefers its lower stems and root area to be cool and in shade. Can be tricky to grow, and either loves or hates your garden. It makes a marvellous summer curtain growing through an evergreen hedge such as yew. Zones 8–11

***Uncinia rubra* (hook sedge):** Evergreen perennial with 3-angled stems and long, shiny, greenish-red or reddish-brown leaves. Dark brown or almost black spikes of flowers are produced in summer. Height 12in, spread 16in. Dislikes prolonged periods of frost. Grow in moist but well-drained soil in sun or light shade. Zones 8–11

***Verbascum bombyciferum* (mullein):** Short-lived evergreen perennial with large, white-woolly, basal leaves. The spikes of saucer-shaped, bright yellow flowers appear in summer. Height 8ft, spread 20in. May be wind-damaged in an exposed position. Grow in infertile, well-drained, gritty soil in full sun. Useful where summer height is needed and the site is small: many of the mulleins will grow to 6ft or more by early summer. It is advisable to remove the dead flower heads, to prevent thousands of seeds from being scattered through the garden and growing like weeds. Zones 5–9

***Verbena bonariensis*:** Perennial with stiff, upright, deep green branching stems and mid-green, lance-shaped leaves. The panicles of small, pink-purple flowers are produced from midsummer until fall. Height 6ft, spread 16in. Grow in moist, well-drained, fertile soil in full sun. Ideal for growing up through medium-height spring-flowering shrubs with an open habit of growth. Will self-seed readily. Zones 7–11

# Best dozen bulbs for the small garden

**Allium cernuum (nodding onion):** Bulbous perennial with pungent, strap-like, dark green basal leaves. The pendant umbels of up to 30 bell-shaped, deep pink flowers appear on stiff, upright stems in summer. Height 16–20in, spread 3in. Grow in fertile, well-drained soil in full sun. Zones 4–8

*Allium schoenoprasum* (edible chives) make an attractive low, pale purple flowering edge to a path or perennial border. Zones 4–11

**Anemone blanda 'Atrocaerulea' (windflower):** Tuberous perennial with dark green leaves. The solitary, deep blue, daisy-like flowers appear above the leaves in late winter and early spring. Height and spread 6in. Grow in well-drained, humus-rich soil in sun or light shade. They quickly spread, forming an early carpet of color, dying down long before summer. Zones 4–8

**Crocus tommasinianus:** Cormous perennial with thin, strap-like, mid-green leaves which appear at the same time as the flowers, becoming longer after flowering. Up to two slender, pale lilac to rose-purple flowers appear in late winter and early spring. Height 2.5–3in, spread 1in. Grow in free-draining, gritty, fertile soil in full sun. Suitable for naturalising in grass, where it will quickly spread by seed and offsets. Zones 3–8

**Cyclamen hederifolium:** Tuberous perennial with mid- to dark green leaves usually purple-green on the underside. The reflexed flowers, in shades of pink with small, deep maroon blotches at the base of each petal, appear before the leaves in mid- to late fall. Height 4–5in, spread 6in. Grow in well-drained, humus-rich, fertile soil in light shade. Self-seeds freely, slowly forming a carpet of fall color. Ideal for planting under trees. Zones 5–7

**Erythronium 'Pagoda' (trout lily):** Bulbous perennial with a long, tooth-like bulb and long mid-green foliage mottled with bronzy purple. In spring, 12–14in-tall stems of 2–5 bright yellow flowers appear. The flower petals have a brown base and the anthers are a darker yellow. The plant spread is 4in. Plant in a deep, woodsy-type soil in light to partial shade. Soak purchased bulbs for 24 hours before planting. Trout lilies are also available in white, pink, or mauve. Zones 4–9.

**Fritillaria michailovskyi:** Bulbous perennial with lance-shaped, mid-green leaves and umbels of bell-shaped, pendant brown-purple early summer flowers tinged green, with yellow tepal (petal-like) tips. Height 6–8in, spread 2in. Dislikes wet ground when dormant in winter. Grow in well-drained, gritty, fertile soil in full sun. An unusual species that is ideal for growing in a well-drained rock garden soil or growing in a window box. Zones 4–8

**Galanthus nivalis (snowdrop):** Bulbous perennial with slightly twisted, glaucous leaves and scented, pure white flowers in winter and early spring. Each one has long green ovaries behind the flower and two

TOP: *Allium cernuum (nodding onion).*
BOTTOM: *Crocus tommasinianus.*

green marks on the inner tepals. Height 4in, spread 2in. Grow in moist but well-drained, humus-rich soil in partial shade. Every garden should have snowdrops, if only to let you know that spring is just around the corner. Zones 3–8

**Hyacinthoides orientalis 'Queen of the Pinks' (hyacinth):** Bulbous perennial with lance-shaped, bright green leaves. The erect racemes of bell-shaped, very fragrant, waxy, deep pink flowers appear in early spring. Height 8–12in, spread 3in. Grow in well-drained soil in sun or light shade. Ideal for growing in shallow containers. If mixed varieties are planted in the same container, they may not all flower at the same time. Zones 4–9

**Iris reticulata 'Cantab':** Bulbous perennial with square-sectioned mid-green leaves. The solitary, pale blue, fragrant flower has deeper blue downward-curving lower petals (called the falls), each with a yellow crest, and appears in late winter. Height 4–6in, spread 2in. Grow in well-drained, neutral-to-alkaline soil in full sun. Suitable for the rock garden, in containers or as a surprise show tucked into some corner of the garden. Zones 4–8

There are many other species of iris, including the magnificent summer-flowering flag iris grown from rhizomes.

**Muscari latifolium (grape hyacinth):** Bulbous perennial with lance-shaped, mid-green leaves. The spring-flowering, dense racemes are made up of small, urn-shaped,

violet-black flowers with pale blue sterile flowers on the upper stem. Height 8in, spread 2in. Grow in moist, well-drained soil in full sun. Ideal in containers, such as window boxes, or planted in pockets in a rock garden. Zones 4–8

**Narcissus bulbocodium (hoop-petticoat daffodil):** Bulbous perennial with narrow, dark green leaves. The funnel-shaped, deep yellow flowers with extra-long trumpets and small, pointed outer petals are produced in mid-spring. Height 4–6in, spread 2in. Grow in moist, well-drained, neutral-to-acid soil in full sun or light shade. Suitable for naturalising in soil that doesn't dry out in summer. Great for containers, edging a border or in a rock garden. Zones 3–9

There many species and varieties of daffodil, but beware of permanent plantings of late-flowering varieties with long leaves, as after flowering the foliage will be unsightly until it dies down.

**Tulipa praestans 'Unicum' (tulip):** Bulbous perennial with gray-green leaves with creamy-white margins. Each stem has a cluster of up to five, bowl-shaped, bright red flowers with yellow bases and blue-black anthers, appearing in early spring. Height 12in, spread 6in. Grow in well-drained soil that is dry in summer. There are legion tulip species and varieties, all of which will enhance the smallest garden. Zones 4–8

TOP: *Fritillaria michailovskyi.*
BOTTOM: *Muscari latifolium (grape hyacinth).*

# Best dozen annuals for maximum impact

*Amaranthus caudatus* **(love-lies-bleeding, tassel flower):** Bushy, erect annual with red or green stems and pale green leaves. The pendant panicles of crimson flowers are tassel-like and 18–24in long during summer and early fall. Height 3–4ft, spread 1.5–2ft. May be raised early from seed and hardened off or sown directly into the ground after frost. A talking point in the garden. It is almost vulgar but makes a spectacular dot plant through a bed of carpeting annuals.

*Callistephus chinensis* **'Ostrich Plume' (China aster):** Annual with mid-green leaves. The long stems support reflexed, feathery, double flower heads in shades of white, pink, red, and blue during summer and fall. Height 20in, spread 12in. Plant out after last frost. Grow in fertile, moist, well-drained, neutral-to-alkaline soil in full sun. Makes a great cut flower for indoor decoration.

*Clarkia amoena* **Satin Series (Godetia, satin flower):** Dwarf, bushy annual with dark green leaves. The single flowers are available in pastel shades with white margins or in contrasting colors and will flower profusely throughout the summer and fall. Height 8in, spread 6in. Grow in impoverished, moist but well-drained acid soil in full sun or light shade.

*Datura inoxia* **(angel's trumpet):** Tender perennial grown as an annual with large, mid-green leaves. The highly fragrant, 8in-long, trumpet-shaped flowers are a very pale shade of lilac, almost white but not quite. They point upwards, flowering from summer through to the first frost. Height and spread 3ft. Plant out after all risk of frost is over. Grow in free-draining, humus-rich soil in a sheltered, sunny position. Ideal as a perfumed patio plant in a large container for the summer months.

*Dianthus chinensis* **'Black and White Minstrels' (Chinese pink):** Short-lived perennial usually grown annually from seed. The thin, pale green leaves almost disappear when the white-margined, deep maroon flowers appear in summer. The scent is strong and sweet. Height 10–12in, spread 6–8in. Grow in well-drained soil in full sun. Good in hanging baskets or as a summer-flowering dwarf edging along paths.

*Dorotheanthus bellidiformis* **(Mesembryanthemum, Livingstone daisy):** Annual with spoon-shaped, fleshy, light green leaves. The solitary, daisy-like flowers appear during summer in a range of bright colors, some with contrasting colors towards the centers. Height 4in, spread 12in. Plant out after all risk of frost is past. Grow in an impoverished, sandy, free-draining soil in full sun. Produces a carpet of bright colors, but the flowers will close up in shade or in dull weather.

*Helianthus annuus* **'Big Smile' (sunflower):** Hairy-stemmed annual with mid- to dark green, hairy leaves. The 4in-diameter, daisy-like bright yellow flowers have dark yellow disc-florets in the center. Height

TOP: *Callistephus chinensis 'Ostrich Plume'.*
BOTTOM: *Dorotheanthus bellidiformis (Mesembryanthemum, Livingstone daisy).*

18in, spread 12in. Plant out after all risk of frost is past. Grow in humus-rich, alkaline, well-drained soil in a sheltered position in full sun.

It is dads who love to grow the 'Russian Giant' varieties of sunflower that manage to reach 10–12ft; children love the dwarf varieties that they can see and appreciate!

***Lathyrus odoratus* Galaxy Group (sweet pea):** Annual climber with winged stems and mid- to dark green leaves. The racemes of up to 7–8 wavy-edged, white, pink, scarlet or blue flowers have a strong fragrance and are produced from summer to fall. Height 6–7ft. Will need supporting trellis or wire mesh that the tendrils can cling to. Young plants produced under cover need to be hardened off before being planted outside. Grow in deep, moisture-retentive, well-drained, humus-rich soil in full sun. Ideal as a summer screen for privacy on the patio. Excellent as a cut flower for filling a room with fragrance.

***Matthiola incana* Cinderella Series (gillyflower, stock):** Woody-based perennial usually grown as an annual from seed. The leaves are pale green or gray-green. The racemes of fragrant double flowers are white or shades of pink, red, and blue. Height and spread 10in. Harden off before planting out in a sheltered position after the last frost. Grow in moist, well-drained, neutral-to-alkaline soil in full sun. Ideal for containers on the patio or to welcome visitors at the front door. Makes a good cut flower if the leaves are removed.

***Nemesia strumosa* 'KLM':** Branching annual with mid-green leaves and terminal racemes of 2-lipped, bicolour flowers in white and blue with yellow throats. Height 6–12in, spread 6in. Sow under cover and plant out after all risk of frost is over. Grow in moist, well-drained, slightly acid soil in full sun. Avoid soil that dries out in summer, otherwise flower production will stop.

***Nicotiana sylvestris* (tobacco plant):** Annual with dark green leaves. The tall stems produce panicles of long-tubed, trumpet-shaped, highly fragrant, pure white flowers during summer. Height 4–5ft, spread 20in. Sow seed or plant out after all risk of frost is over. Grow in fertile, moist, well-drained soil in partial shade. The flowers close in full sun. *Sylvestris* means "of the woods"—hence the shade.

***Rudbeckia hirta* 'Bambi' (black-eyed Susan):** Short-lived perennial grown as an annual with mid-green leaves. The daisy-like flower heads are bronze and chestnut-brown with bright yellow ray-florets in the center during summer and early fall. Height and spread 12in. Grow in heavy but well-drained soil in sun or light shade. It is essential that the soil doesn't dry out in summer or flowering will cease.

Top: *Nicotiana sylvestris (tobacco plant).*
Bottom: *Rudbeckia hirta 'Bambi' (black-eyed Susan).*

# Index

# Picture Credits

MMGI: Marianne Majerus Garden Images
GPL: Garden Picture Library
GC: Garden Collection
GAP: GAP Photos

t = top
b = bottom
m = middle
l = left
r = right

page 1 Friedrich Strauss/GPL; 2 Marianne Majerus/MMGI; 5 (t) John Glover/GAP (m) Janet Seaton/GPL (b) Mel Watson/GAP; 6 Sunniva Harte/GPL; 7 (l) Jinny Blom/GAP (b) John Glover/GAP; 8 (t) Pernilla Bergdahl/GAP (b) Sarah Layton/GAP

**Chapter 1: What have you got?**
page 11 Jonathan Buckley; 12 Jacqui Hurst/GPL; 13 Susanna Jahn/GAP; 14 (l) Howard Rice/GPL (r) Blanche Baron/MMGI; 15 Marie Brandolini/MMGI; 17 John Glover/GAP; 18 Jason Samlley/GAP; 19 Marianne Majerus/MMGI

**Chapter 2: What do you want?**
page 20 Jerry Harpur/GAP (designer Luciano Giubelei); 22 (t) Jerry Harpur/GAP (b) Jonathan Buckley; 23 (top) Tim Gainey/GAP (b) Jo Whitworth/GAP; 24 Juliette Wade/GPL; 25 Jonathan Buckley; 27 Claire Davies/GAP

**Chapter 3: Landscaping your space**
page 28 Juliette Wade/GAP; 30 Mark Bolton/GPL; 31 Lynne Brotchie/GPL; 32 (l) Jilayne Rickards/MMGI (m) Mel Watson/GAP (r) Janet Seaton/GPL; 33 Mel Watson/GAP; 34 Martin Hughes-Jones/GWI; 35 Pearson Victoria/GPL; 36 Zara Napier/GAP; 37 (l) Marianne Majerus/MMGI (r) Jonathan Buckley; 38 (l) Marijke Heuff/GPL (r) Howard Rice/GPL; 39 (l) Andrea Jones/GAP (r) Jonathan Buckley; 40 Janet Seaton/GPL; 41 Linda Burgess/GPL; 42 John Glover/GAP; 43 Jill Billington/MMGI; 44 Maddie Thornhill/GAP; 45 Neil Holmes/GAP; p 47 Steven Wooster/GPL

**Chapter 4: Choosing plants**
page 48 Graham Strong/GPL; 50 (l) Graham Strong/GAP (r) Jilayne Rickards/MMGI; 51 Leigh Clapp/GAP; 52 (tl) John Glover/GAP (tr) Lynn Keddie/GPL (bl) Leigh Clapp/GAP (br) Geoff Kidd/GAP; 53 (tl) Alec Scaresbrook/GPL (tr) Marianne Majerus/MMGI (bl) Geoff Kidd/GAP (br) Clive Nichols/GAP; 55 Elke Borkowski/GAP; 56 Richard Bloom/GAP; 57 Mark Bolton/GAP; 58 (l) GAP (r) John Glover/GAP; 59 (l) Carole Drake/GAP (r) Howard Rice/GPL; 60

(t) Mark Bolton/GAP (b) Elke Burkowski/GAP; 61 Marianne Majerus/MMGI; 62 Codie Coniguaro/GAP; 64 J S Sira/GAP; 65 Neil Holmes/GPL; 66 (t) Elke Burkowski/GAP (b) Graham Strong/GAP; 67 (t) Rob Whitworth/GAP (b) Jerry Pavia/GPL; 68 (t) John Glover/GAP (b) Hemant Jariwala/GPL; 69 (t) J S Sira/GAP (b) Jo Whitworth/GAP; 70 Graham Strong/GAP; 71 (t) Mark Bolton/GAP (b) Victoria Fimston/GAP; 72 Graham Strong/GAP; 74 Dominique Lubar/MMGI; 75 (l) Carole Drake/GPL (r) Lynne Brotchie/GPL; 76 Ruth Collier/MMGI; 77 Francois De Heel/GPL; 78 Jonathan Buckley; 79 (l) Geoff Kidd/GAP (r) Richard Bloom/GAP; 80 J S Sira/GPL; 81 Aaron McCoy/GPL; 82 (l) Marianne Majerus/MMGI (r) Graham Strong/GAP; 83 Jill Billington/MMGI; 84 (tl) Clive Nichols/GAP (bl) Lynn Keddie/GAP; 85 (tr) Friedrich Strauss/GPL (br) Tudor Spencer/MMGI; 86 Neil Sutherland/GC; 87 (l) Graham Strong/GAP (r) Geoff Kidd/GAP; 88 John Glover/GAP; 89 Lynn Keddie/GAP

**Chapter 5: Designing**
page 90 Marcus Harpur/GAP; 92 (r) Mark Bolton/GAP; 93 (t and br) Leigh Clapp/GAP (bl) Steven Wooster/GPL; 94 Mark Bolton/GAP; 95 (l) Mark Bolton/GAP (r) Elke Burkowski/GAP; 96 Mark Bolton/GAP; 97 Steven Wooster/GPL; 98 Janet Seaton/GPL; 99 Jonathan Buckley; 100 Flora Press/GPL; 103 Premium Stock/GAP; 104 Jonathan Buckley/GAP

**Chapter 6: Case studies**
page 106 Nicola Browne/GAP; 108 Rob Whitworth/GAP; 110 (l) Jo Whitworth/GPL (r) Marcus Whitworth/GAP; 112 (l) FhF Greenmedia/GAP (r) Nic Hamilton/Alamy; 114 (l) Rob Whitworth/GAP (r) Howard Rice/GAP; 116 (t) Lynn Keddie/GAP (b) Neil Holmes/GAP; 118 (t) J S Sira/GPL (b) Marcus Harpur/GAP

**Chapter 7: Construction**
page 121 Mark Winwood/GPL; 122 Mel Watson/GAP; 123 Marianne Majerus/MMGI; 125 Mark Winwood/GPL; 126–127 Marianne Majerus/MMGI; 128 GAP Photos/Rice/Buckland; 130 (t) Stephen and Ruth Kersley/MMGI (b) Elke Burkowski/GAP; 131 Elke Burkowski/GAP; 133 Clive Nichols/GAP; 135 FhF Greenmedia/GAP; 136 Elke Burkowsk/GAP; 137 Marianne Majerus/MMGI

**Chapter 8: Planting, growing and nurturing your garden**
page 138 Agencja Free/GAP; 141 Janet Johnson/GAP; 143 (l) Photos Lamontagne/GPL (r) Liz Eddison/GC; 144 Paul Debois/GAP; 145 Baigrie James/GPL; 146 Howard Rice/GAP; 147 Visions/GAP;

149 Marianne Majerus/MMGI; 151 Friedrich Strauss/GAP; 152 (l) Marianne Majerus/MMGI (r) Richard Bloom/GAP; 153 Geoff Kidd/GAP; 154 Maxine Adcock/GAP; 155 Dave Bevan/GWI; 156 Francesca Yorke/GPL; 157 (l) Martin Hughes-Jones/GWI (m) Claire Davies/GPL (r) Trevor Sims/GWI; 158 Nigel Cattlin/Alamy; 159 (l) John Swithinbank/GWI (m) Photos Lamontagne/GPL (r) Neil Holmes/GPL

**Appendix—Plant directory**
page 161 (t) Martin Page/GPL (b) Lynn Keddie/GPL; 162 Richard Bloom/GPL; 163 (t) J S Sira/GPL (b) Howard Rice/GPL; 164 Botanica/GPL; 165 (t) Richard Bloom/GPL (b) Howard Rice/GPL; 166 (t) Howard Rice/GPL (b) J S Sira/GPL; 167 Don Johnston/Alamy; 168 Mark Bolton/GPL; 169 (t) J S Sira/GPL (b) Zara Napier/GAP; 170 (t) Christie Carter/GPL (b) Richard Bloom/GAP; 171 Christina Bollen/GAP; 172 (t) John Glover/GAP (b) Howard Rice/GPL; 173 Mark Bolton/GPL; 174 (t) Anne Hyde/GPL (b) Pernilla Bergdahl/GPL; 175 J S Sira/GPL; 176 Sunniva Harte/GPL; 177 (t) Ron Evans/GPL (b) John Glover/GPL; 178 (t) John Glover/GPL (b) Chris Burrows/GPL; 179 John Glover/GPL; 180 (t) Wildscape/Alamy (b) Stephen Shepherd/GPL; 181 Richard Bloom/GPL; 182 (t) Tracey Rich/GPL (b) Lynn Keddie/GPL; 183 Martin Page/GPL; 184 (t and b) Hemant Jariwala/GPL; 185 (t) Mark Bolton/GPL (b) James Guilliam/GPL; 186 (t) Michael Davis/GPL (b) Chris Burrows/GPL; 187 (t) Botanica/GPL (b) Turner Mark/GPL

## ACKNOWLEDGEMENTS
A big thank you to Jenny Wheatley for pulling everything together and to Penny Phillips for whipping the text into shape. My thanks also go to Julia Gelpke for locating some wonderful images, and to Louise Leffler for creating such a stylish book. And to Kyle, as always, for her continued support.